TOWARD
AN
AESTHETICS
OF THE
PUPPET

Recent Titles in
Contributions in Drama and Theatre Studies

From Stanislavsky to Barrault: Representative Directors of the
European Stage
Samuel L. Leiter

On Playing Shakespeare: Advice and Commentary from Actors and
Actresses of the Past
Leigh Woods

Eugene O'Neill's Century: Centennial Views on America's Foremost
Tragic Dramatist
Richard F. Moorton, Jr., editor

Strategies of Drama: The Experience of Form
Oscar Lee Brownstein

Radical Stages: Alternative History in Modern British Drama
D. Keith Peacock

A Search for a Postmodern Theater: Interviews with
Contemporary Playwrights
John L. DiGaetani

The Age of *Hair:* Evolution and Impact of Broadway's First Rock Musical
Barbara Lee Horn

The Gymnasium of the Imagination: A Collection of Children's Plays in
English, 1780–1860
Jonathan Levy

Every Week, A Broadway Revue: The Tamiment Playhouse, 1921–1960
Martha Schmoyer LoMonaco

The Simple Stage: Origins of the Minimalist *Mise-en-Scène* in the
American Theater
Arthur Feinsod

Richard's Himself Again: A Stage History of *Richard III*
Scott Colley

Eugene O'Neill In China: An International Centenary Celebration
Haiping Liu and Lowell Swortzell, editors

TOWARD AN AESTHETICS OF THE PUPPET

PUPPETRY AS A THEATRICAL ART

Steve Tillis

CONTRIBUTIONS IN DRAMA AND THEATRE STUDIES,
NUMBER 47

GREENWOOD PRESS

New York

Westport, Connecticut

London

Library of Congress Cataloging-in-Publication Data

Tillis, Steve.

    Toward an aesthetics of the puppet : puppetry as a theatrical art
/ Steve Tillis.

      p.   cm. — (Contributions in drama and theatre studies, ISSN
0163-3821 ; no. 47)

    Includes bibliographical references and index.

    ISBN 0-313-28359-1 (alk. paper)

    1. Puppet theater. 2. Aesthetics. I. Title. II. Series.

PN1972.T56   1992

791.5'3'01 — dc20   91-43366

British Library Cataloguing in Publication Data is available.

Library of Congress Catalog Card Number: 91–43366

ISBN: 0-313-28359-1

ISSN: 0163–3821

First published in 1992

Greenwood Press, 88 Post Road West, Westport, CT 06881
An imprint of Greenwood Publishing Group, Inc.

Printed in the United States of America

The paper used in this book complies with the
Permanent Paper Standard issued by the National
Information Standards Organization (Z39.48-1984).

P

In order to keep this title in print and available to the academic community, this edition
was produced using digital reprint technology in a relatively short print run. This would
not have been attainable using traditional methods. Although the cover has been changed
from its original appearance, the text remains the same and all materials and methods
used still conform to the highest book-making standards.

Copyright Acknowledgments

The author and publisher are grateful to the following for allowing the use of materials:

Used with permission of Marjorie Batchelder McPharlin. *Rod-Puppets and the Human Theatre*. Columbus: Ohio State University Press, 1947.

Paul McPharlin, "Aesthetics of the Puppet Revival." Unpublished master's thesis, Wayne State University.

Frank Proschan, "Puppet Voices and Interlocutors: Language in Folk Puppetry." Reproduced by permission of the American Folklore Society from the *Journal of American Folklore* 94: 374, Oct-Dec. 1981. Not for further reproduction.

Dezso Szilágyi, ed., *Contemporary Hungarian Puppet Theatre*. Budapest: Corvina Books, 1978.

Petr Bogatyrev, "The Interconnection of Two Similar Semiotic Systems: The Puppet Theatre and the Theatre of Living Actors," translated by Milanne S. Hahn, in *Semiotica,* 47-1/4 (1983): 47–68.

Jiri Veltrusky, "Puppetry and Acting," *Semiotica* 47-1/4 (1983): 69–122.

Thomas A. Green and W. J. Pepicello, "Semiotic Interrelationships in the Puppet Play," *Semiotica* 47-1/4 (1983): 147–61.

Frank Proschan, "The Semiotic Study of Puppets, Masks, and Performing Objects," *Semiotica* 47-1/4 (1983): 3–44.

The Puppet Theatre of the Modern World, edited by UNIMA (l'Union Internationale de la Marionnette) and Margaret Niculescu, translated by Ewald Osers and Elizabeth Strick. Plays, Inc., 1967.

James R. Brandon, ed., *On Thrones of Gold: Three Javanese Shadow Plays*. Harvard University Press, 1970.

Henryk Jurkowski, "The Sign Systems of Puppetry." In *Aspects of the Puppet Theatre,* co-translator and editor Penny Francis. London: Puppet Centre Trust, 1988.

Conrad Aiken, *Collected Poems*. New York: Oxford University Press, 1964.

Every reasonable effort has been made to trace the owners of copyright materials in this book, but in some instances this has proven impossible. The author and publisher will be glad to receive information leading to more complete acknowledgments in subsequent printings of the book and in the meantime extend their apologies for any omissions.

To my maternal grandfather, Jacob Gelfand

CONTENTS

PREFACE

I became involved with puppets not through any childhood interest, but through my employment with Dr. Edison's Traveling Medicine Show, a vagabond troupe with whom I threw my lot many years ago. That show has since ceased traveling, but my involvement with puppets has continued, for many years as a performer, and now, it seems, as a scholar. Over those years I have taken on many debts, which I cannot fully repay, but will gladly acknowledge.

Toby Grace, the late Ray Nelson, Bob Brown, Ken Moses, and Bart P. Roccoberton, Jr., directors of estimable touring companies, taught me most of what I know about puppet performance; without their assistance, I could not have begun this study. Bob Brown was also kind enough to allow me access to his personal library. Cheryl Koehler and Carol Wolfe, experienced puppet-artists, tolerated discussion of many of the ideas presented here.

Karl Toepfer, David Kahn, and Ethel Walker, professors at San Jose State University, taught me most of what I know about scholarly writing; without their assistance, I could not have completed this study. Karl Toepfer also served as my M.A. advisor, and was Virgil to my Dante in the arcane world of literary and dramatic theory.

Lou Furman, of Washington State University, and Dorlis Grubidge, of the University of Wisconsin, Oshkosh, offered useful criticism and provided vital encouragement. I also received encouragement from

Henryk Jurkowski, the world's premier scholar of puppetry. The reader will soon note that I disagree with Professor Jurkowski on a number of issues. When I had occasion to warn him of these disagreements, he gently replied, "Ah, but we are scholars. We're *supposed* to disagree." Whatever issues may separate us, my comprehension of puppetry would have remained impoverished without the stimulation provided by learning from and disagreeing with Professor Jurkowski.

Marilyn Brownstein, Maureen Melino, Kellie Cardone, Ruth Adkins, and Susan Baker, all from Greenwood Press, labored mightily with my ragged manuscript; without their assistance, and the assistance of their many colleagues, I would not have been able to offer the reader a presentable book.

Finally, it is with the greatest pleasure that I take this opportunity to thank my wife, Adrienne Baker, for her unstinting support of every kind, and for her unshakable faith that I might, someday, have something useful to say. And I would also like to thank our son, Sam Tillis, for having had the decency to take very regular, and extended, naps.

I alone am responsible for whatever foolishness the reader finds in this book.

TOWARD
AN
AESTHETICS
OF THE
PUPPET

INTRODUCTION

Puppets have been used in theatrical performance around the world and far back into history. Every inhabited continent boasts its own puppet traditions, be they associated with tribal or village cultures, with developed civilizations, or with both. But despite their ubiquity, puppets have received little attention in the theoretical study of the theatre.

This book will address fundamental problems in theatrical puppetry, with the intent of establishing the theoretical basis and descriptive vocabulary for a general aesthetics of the puppet. The scope of these problems, and the approach to be taken in addressing them, will be explained later in this introduction; but it will be best to begin with some evidence of the vast range of puppet-performance.

In Nigeria, members of the Ibabio tribe assemble by day in an open, sandy area. Before them are blankets, sewn one to another and hung from wooden rails; above this wall of blankets are one-foot-tall figures of men and women, each constructed of a few pieces of sculpted and painted wood. The figures seem to move and speak for themselves; in fact, they are moved via sets of rods, and the speech given them is distorted and unnatural. They perform bawdy and comic scenes of "topical events drawn from tribal culture . . . [including] scenes of domestic life as well as a number of satirical references to the prevailing systems of tribal and colonial government" (Malkin 1977: 64–65; see also Proschan 1980: 24, and Messenger 1971: 208).

In Java, villagers sit in the cool of the night to celebrate some local event. At the place of celebration, a large screen of white cotton cloth is stretched within a wooden frame, and behind it is a burning lamp; but the word "behind" is without real meaning, for the villagers sit on both sides of the screen. Between the screen and the lamp are, variously, figures of men, women, gods, animals, even whole marching armies; these figures are elaborately cut and painted pieces of cured water-buffalo hide, and range in height from half a foot to four feet tall. Most of the audience watch the shadows these figures cast, while the rest watch the figures themselves, and can see that these figures are given motion, via rods, by a single person, who also gives speech, variously differentiated but without unnatural distortion, to the vast array of figures. Accompanying music is nearly continuous, providing background accompaniment, song, and occasional foreground respite from the action. The figures perform a mythological story, alternately comic, tragic, and heroic, concerning the gods; the performance is an integral part of the celebration, and will last from sundown to sunrise (Brandon 1970: 35–69; Ulbricht 1970: 5–14).

These are disparate examples of dramatic theatre: the Nigerian performance was witnessed early in this century, and derives from a tradition that our references imply is long-lived, but do not trace back in time; the Javanese performance occurred in the 1960's, and is derived from a tradition of puppetry dating back perhaps to the ninth century, and certainly to the eleventh century (Brandon 1970: 3). The performances share the peculiarity of presenting objects as if they were alive. The common word for such theatrical figures is "puppet."

In London, England, an assortment of people taking their leisure in Regent's Park gather together before an oblong tent, six feet high, with an opening in its front. Within that opening are one-foot-tall figures of a hunchbacked man and his wife, both constructed of cloth and wood, both seeming to move and speak of their own accord; in fact, they are given movement and speech by a single man hidden inside the tent. The speech of the wife is a shrill but clear falsetto, while the speech of the hunchback is distorted and unnatural; the wife repeats the hunchback's words so that they can be comprehended. The hunchback will, at various points in the performance, throw his baby out a window, kill a policeman, and confront the devil; this is a comedy (Speaight 1990 [1955]: 208–18).

In Washington, D.C., schoolchildren have been brought by the busload to the Kennedy Center for the Performing Arts; on the vast stage before them are oversized sections of a house and garden, and behind these scenic units stand three vocalists, joined by the National Symphony Orchestra. A singing actor represents a child, while various figures serve as the child's mother and as characters of the child's fantasy life. The figure of the mother is ten feet tall, and constructed of natural and man-made fibers; she is moved via poles and rods through the obvious exertions of two operators, and is given speech by one of the vocalists. The fantasy characters, including the numbers one through nine, are constructed of foam rubber; they are visibly manhandled by their operators and given speech by the remaining vocalists. The speech of each character is as natural as possible, given the strictures of opera. The turning point of the performance is an argument between mother and child, and the child's subsequent refuge in the world of fantasy.

Again, these examples of dramatic theatre are quite disparate. The English performance, a "Punch and Judy" show by Percy Press, Jr., took place in 1977, and derives directly from a puppet tradition going back to the seventeenth century, and indirectly from a live theatre tradition that might be traced all the way to ancient Rome (Baird 1965: 95). The American performance occurred in 1981, under the direction of Bob Brown, and derives from no single tradition, but rather, incorporates diverse practices of the contemporary theatre. Nonetheless, they also share the peculiarity of presenting the theatrical figures known as puppets.

In Rajasthan State, India, villagers are attracted in the evening to the steps of the local temple by the arrival of a subcaste of entertainers, who stretch a brightly colored cloth between two poles and place a lamp at each end of the cloth. In front of the cloth sits one of the entertainers, beating a drum; also in front is suspended, from a bamboo pole, an array of figures, each up to two feet tall, constructed of wood and cloth. When the moment arrives for their use, they are released from the pole and swung into action, their movements obviously controlled by strings that run from them to persons standing above. Their speech is no more than noise, but the noise is carefully articulated, and the drummer serves as translator, making plain what is suggested by it. The figures in action are an idiot clown and a girl who transforms herself into an ogre; they perform a comic tale of love gone wrong (Baird 1965: 46–55; Samar 1960: 64–70).

In Osaka, Japan, people from within and without the city visit an elaborate hall dedicated to a unique style of theatre. On a broad stage is a low platform, behind which is scenery and a painted backdrop; at one end of the platform sit two men, a narrator and a musician. Upon the platform are figures of a man and a woman; these figures, constructed of many pieces of sculpted and painted wood, are gorgeously costumed and bewigged, and are up to five feet tall. Three men are visible behind each of them, obviously giving them movement via hands-on contact and rods. The speech for the figures is provided in a stylized but natural manner by the narrator, backed by the expressive playing of the musician; the narrator and musician also provide more general narration and music. The figures perform a complex tale that culminates in the suicide of two lovers, a courtesan and an apprentice (Adachi 1985: 12–30).

These last examples are as disparate as any: the Indian performance was witnessed in the 1950's, and derives from a tradition "centuries old" (Baird 1965: 46); the Japanese performance took place in 1977, and derives from a tradition dating to the late sixteenth century (Adachi 1985: 3). They also share the peculiarity of the puppet.

These six examples demonstrate the extraordinary dimensions of the phenomenon of the puppet. Within each of our pairings we see diverse means of performance. Thus, to consider only a limited aspect of performance, our Nigerian example uses rounded figures operated with rods, while the Javanese figures, though also rod-operated, are not rounded but flat, and serve the purpose of casting shadows; our English example uses small figures worn on the hands of their operator, while the American figures are in many cases actually larger than their operators; our Indian example uses simple figures operated from above by a few strings, while the Japanese figures are so elaborately constructed and articulated that they each require up to three operators.

Further, within each of our pairings we see diverse cultural contexts of performance. Thus, our Nigerian, English, and Indian examples are relatively straightforward manifestations of popular culture, while those from Java, America, and Japan are far more complex performances that aspire, and are taken, to be art.

These are only six examples. Countless other examples could, but need not, be set forth, for by themselves these six demonstrate the dimensions of the phenomenon under examination: employing various means, based in popular culture or in sophisticated art, the theatrical figure known as the puppet spans history and geography.

This book, however, will not examine puppetry as it is historically or geographically manifested in any particular culture. Studies of puppetry in some, although not nearly enough, cultures are already available, and frequently succeed in demonstrating traditional uses of the puppet. Neither will this book summarize these studies, and present a history and geography of the puppet. Such general summaries are also available, but tend to ignore the theoretical problems involved in comparing and contrasting puppet performances. We will, however, concern ourselves with the broad range of puppet activity, in an attempt to discover what is constant, and what is variable, across all boundaries of time and space.

Furthermore, this book will not examine the technical practices of puppetry, such as means of construction and presentation. Manuals concerning the appropriate techniques for many, although not all, styles of puppetry are already available, and frequently succeed in explaining how to construct and present the puppets in each instance. Neither will this book summarize these manuals, and present a guide to the practical mechanics of the puppet theatre. Such general summaries are also available, but tend to be oblivious to any problems of theory. We will, however, concern ourselves with the manner in which puppets are made to perform, in an attempt to discover what is constant, and what is variable, in the possibilities of puppet performance.

The phenomenon of the puppet also exists in a variety of contexts that are distinguishable across the boundaries of history and geography, and that make use of all of the technical means available to puppetry.

This book, however, will not examine the puppet as it is found in the context of religion, where it serves as an object of ritual or of sacred presence. Nor will it examine the puppet as it is found in the context of education, where it serves as a tool of learning or of constructive play. Nor, finally, will it examine the puppet as it is found in the context of therapy, where it serves as an agent of healing or of self-exploration. Discussion of puppetry in any of these contexts is tangential to our immediate concern, which is puppetry in the context of the theatre, where it serves primarily to entertain. Our discussion might prove useful in the examination of puppetry in these other contexts, but such utility must be left for others to work out.

This book, then, is dedicated to cross-cultural observation and analysis of theatrical puppet performance; or, to put it another way, it is dedicated to addressing the fundamental grounds of puppetry as a theatrical art. Thus, our central theoretical problem is: how are we to comprehend and describe the phenomenon of the puppet as it is presented in its various theatrical manifestations?

Having already circumscribed the limitations of this book so severely, we must circumscribe them even further, for the complexities of puppet performance are such that there will not be space to address any problem other than those arising from the puppet itself. Thus, such problems as exist in the relationships of the puppet with the performance text, with associated music, with metatextual characters, and even, to a large degree, with the puppet-artist(s), must be left to future study.

Our problem here is with the puppet itself. Addressing this problem will require scrupulous attention, and though such attention is not common to writing about puppetry, it is not unknown; indeed, one may even say it is hallowed by time. An ancient reference to Javanese puppet theatre can be found in the *Meditation of Ardjuna*, composed by the court poet of King Airlangga (A.D. 1035–1049):

> There are people who weep, are sad and aroused watching puppets, though they know they are merely carved pieces of leather manipulated and made to speak. These people are like men who, thirsting for sensuous pleasures, live in a world of illusion; they do not realize the magic hallucinations they see are not real. (quoted in Brandon 1970: 3)

The basic elements of puppetry, elements that are constant through all of the examples given earlier, are noted in this remarkable passage: the designed figure, the movement and the speech given to that figure, and the audience that knows the figure to be an instrument of theatre, and yet participates in the illusion it creates.

Let us look for a moment at the elements associated with the puppet itself that make possible the response of the audience. The examination of these elements may be said to be a study of the semiotics of the puppet, a study of the signs by which the puppet communicates.

As the passage quoted above suggests, and our earlier examples demonstrate, three types of signs make up, or constitute, the puppet: signs of design, of movement, and of speech. One may say that these signs, whatever their specific nature, arise from the general sign-systems of design, movement, and speech. The specific signs that constitute the puppet are related to signs that are generally recognized as signs of life; that is, as signs one associates with the presence of life. To give a simple example: the puppet might have a mouth, as living beings have mouths; the mouth might be made to open and close, as the mouths of living beings open and close; and associated with the mouth might be the suggested delivery of speech, as living beings deliver speech. But when these signs are presented by the puppet, they no longer signify the actual presence of life. The signs have been abstracted from life, and are now presented by something without life of its own.

It is in response to the signs deployed by the puppet, signs that normally signify life, that the audience accords the puppet its spurious life. The study of this dynamic relationship between the puppet and its audience may be said to be a study of the phenomenology of the puppet, a study of the phenomenon of puppet performance as a distinctive theatrical event.

This book will follow the example of the court poet of Airlangga and attempt to comprehend the puppet by examining how the deployment of abstracted signs creates an illusion of life that the audience knows is not real, and will develop a concept called double-vision, which postulates that an audience sees the puppet in two ways at one time: as a perceived object and as an imagined life.

The theoretical problems of the puppet will be directly addressed. Thus, Part I asks: how is the puppet to be defined; or, what is to be considered a puppet? It also asks: how is the puppet to be explained; or, what is the basis of the puppet's appeal through its historic and geographic diversity? After discussing the standard solutions to these problems in Chapters 1 and 2, new solutions will be developed and applied in Chapter 3. Part II of this book asks: how is the puppet to be described; or, what taxonomic theory offers a satisfactory framework for comparing and contrasting various puppet performances? Chapter 4 discusses the standard solutions to this problem, while in Chapter 5, a new solution will be developed and applied. As a coda to this study, the use of the word "puppet" as a metaphor will be examined, for the power of such metaphoric usage is strikingly illuminated by the solutions we will advance.

This book is intended for a hybrid audience, on the premise that puppet practice can inform theatrical scholarship, while, conversely, theatrical scholarship can enrich puppet practice. Thus, this book is written both for scholars of the theatre and for practitioners of puppetry, with the hope that members of each group will learn, from their own perspectives, of puppetry as a theatrical art; it is also written for the general public, some of whose members may be curious about this ubiquitous, if frequently disdained, form of theatre. Specialists may find that too much space has been devoted to matters with which they are already familiar; scholars, however, must understand that many readers will lack acquaintance with such concepts as semiotics and phenomenology, while practitioners must acknowledge that many readers will have little awareness of the complexities of puppet performance. Readers who are neither scholars nor practitioners are perhaps the most important part of our audience, for they are, ultimately, the people whom scholars strive to enlighten, and practitioners struggle to entertain. These readers must be allowed enough detailed information, clearly purveyed, to come to grips with both the theoretical and practical aspects of puppetry.

The general approach of this book will be, to borrow terms from the field of linguistics, synchronic, as opposed to diachronic. A diachronic approach, the study of a subject through its historic and geographic development with due consideration to the details of its technical practices, presupposes that a methodology for such study exists. But as we will see, no satisfactory theory, and no satisfactory vocabulary, have yet been created for the theatrical puppet. A synchronic approach, the study of the underlying principles of a subject, attempts to develop the necessary theory and vocabulary through painstaking observation and analysis, isolating and exploring the fundamental constants and variables of the puppet as it exists in all of its theatrical manifestations. Thus, synchronic study is useful as prologue, extended as it may be, to any rigorous diachronic study.

But is a synchronic approach appropriate to the study of puppetry? Henryk Jurkowski, a Polish scholar and producer who has served with great distinction as secretary general and as president of UNIMA (Union Internationale de la Marionnette), has serious doubts:

> [Such] an approach happens to be applied rather often by contemporary scholars who discuss the characteristics of the puppet theatre. Puppetry for them seems to be a synchronically unified monolith, although contemporary puppet theatre is a rich and differentiated totality, taking in cultural elements of different provenance and from different epochs. (1988 [1983]: 62)

Indeed, the central point of Jurkowski's important essay "The Sign Systems of Puppetry" is that the puppet can be found variously in service of "neighbor sign systems," of the "sign system of the live theatre," of the "sign system of the puppet theatre," and of a theatre based upon "the atomization of all elements of the puppet theatre" (1988 [1983]: 68). Jurkowski argues that synchronic approaches ignore this variety of employments for the puppet, and so inevitably misunderstand the realities of the puppet as it exists in "concrete theatrical epoch[s], determined by territory and cultural tradition" (1988 [1983]: 62).

What is more, even if a synchronic approach were viable, Jurkowski suggests, its value would be minimal:

> If one takes this entire range of puppet theatre as a field of scientific investigation, a preliminary task is to make a register or index of its various elements. . . . This register may be of some use as a demonstration of the puppet theatre's means of expression, but I am afraid it will not tell us much more about puppetry than we know already. (1988 [1983]: 62)

How might one respond to these remarks?

First, the scholar whom Jurkowski cites as the foremost exponent of the synchronic approach, Petr Bogatyrev, never actually undertook any systematic study of the puppet; neither did he create anything more than a most preliminary kind of register or index of puppetry. Bogatyrev implied the usefulness of such endeavors, but the focus of his attention was not on the puppet in itself, but rather on puppetry as a form of folk art (see Bogatyrev 1983 [1973]).

Second, whatever Bogatyrev might or might not have done, to employ a synchronic approach to the puppet is not necessarily to consider puppetry as a "synchronically unified monolith." Certainly some, or even most, discussion of puppetry is guilty of hypostatizing some form of puppetry as a model, or ideal form; indeed, Bogatyrev can be condemned for this. Yet a synchronic approach could proceed with a full awareness of the diachronic, multicultural diversity of the puppet and still seek some understanding of the constants and variables to be found throughout that diversity.

Third, the creation of an index of the puppet's "means of expression" would be of far greater usefulness than Jurkowski allows. It may well be that such an index would tell Jurkowski little more than he knew already. This should not be surprising, since Jurkowski knows as much about puppets as any person alive. But neither should it be surprising that few people, be they practitioners, scholars, or audiences of puppetry, know as much as he, and that they might indeed find value in a work that can make sense of the diachronic diversity of the puppet.

An index of the means of expression available to the puppet will provide us with an adequate vocabulary for the discussion of how particular puppets and puppet traditions create theatre; it will provide the basis for an understanding of the puppet's range of performance practices, and for meaningful comparisons of various puppet performances. Additionally, it will demonstrate the manner in which puppetry is a distinctive form of theatre, a form that pleasurably challenges its audience to consider fundamental questions of what it means to be an object and what it means to have life.

And so, despite Jurkowski's misgivings, our approach will be synchronic. But we must be cautioned by Jurkowski's warning against taking puppetry as a monolithic whole, and challenged by his claim that such an approach can scarcely teach much to anyone.

Whatever disagreements one might have with Jurkowski, no doubt he would agree that the purpose of our study is to assist in the comprehension of the phenomenon of the theatrical puppet. Sergei Obraztsov, arguably the most important puppet-artist of the twentieth century, has written: "We must not forget how many people think [puppetry] is not worth taking seriously, that those who study it are wasting their time" (1967 [1965]: 17). This book will attempt to show that puppetry is indeed worth taking seriously. It is a unique and vital manner of theatrical art, a manner that, by its very nature, leads to a fresh understanding of humanity as the maker and breaker of myths about itself and its world.

I

DEFINING AND EXPLAINING THE PUPPET

1

STANDARD DEFINITIONS

What are people talking about when they talk about puppets? The word "puppet" is immediately comprehensible to everyone familiar with the English language, and no doubt conjures up a definite idea in everyone's mind; after all, almost everyone has observed, at one time or another, a puppet-show, or has heard the word puppet used as a metaphor to describe people in certain circumstances of life. But is there any consistency, from one mind to the next, to these ideas of the puppet that arise from individual observation? The burden of definition is to suggest the common idea, rooted in common observation, that gives meaning to a word. Definitions, however, can be curious things.

The word puppet is a case in point: the puppet has been around for countless centuries, and yet remains without a workable definition. Perhaps, given the puppet's diachronic diversity, and the ensuing diversity of people's observations and ideas, it is, in fact, impossible to define. A. R. Philpott, an English puppet-artist and author, notes that "perfect definition eludes theorists, historians, puppeteers, dictionary-makers" (1969: 209); we will see in this chapter just how elusive perfect definition has been. Yet the effort to develop a workable definition, if not a perfect one, is nonetheless worthwhile, for perhaps there might be discovered, after all, some identifiable commonality to the usages of the word puppet.

Paul McPharlin, the most important twentieth-century American scholar of puppetry, provides the basic etymology of the word in the English language:

> *Puppet* . . . comes from *pupa,* Latin for "girl" or "doll" or "small creature." The *-et* makes it diminutive, a *small* small creature. . . . The word *marionette,* of Italian-French origin, [meaning] "little *little* Mary," does not differ from *puppet* in basic meaning, though it has a double diminutive ending. A comparative newcomer to English, it has struck showmen as having a more elegant look than plain old *puppet.* (1949: 5)

This matter of elegance being the sum of the acknowledged difference between the two words, it will be best to follow contemporary usage and stick with puppet for the general phenomenon under discussion, reserving the term marionette for a particular type of puppet.

Obviously, the definition implicit in this etymology is inadequate; one cannot, however, expect etymology to explain the full and current meaning of a word, owing to linguistic and practical developments over time. Dictionary definitions of the word puppet, however, are scarcely better than that implied by etymology, and are nothing short of risible: "A figure (usually small) representing a human being: a child's doll. . . . A human figure, with jointed limbs moved by means of strings or wires: a marionette" (*Oxford English Dictionary*); "A small figure of a human being, that by means of strings or wires is made to perform mock drama; a marionette" (*Funk and Wagnalls*). Other such definitions, being quite similar, need not be adduced.

What is wrong here? It is not the confusion with the word marionette, which is but a quibble. What is wrong is that regardless of the etymology of the word, a puppet need not be small nor "represent a human being," nor be like a "child's doll," nor be moved "by means of strings or wires," nor "perform [in] mock drama," whatever "mock drama" should be construed to mean.

It is untenable to suggest that these definitions are imprecise because they follow common usage, or misusage, for it is quite common to hear of, and to see, large puppets, puppets that represent animals, puppets that are highly sophisticated, and so on. Whatever the reasoning behind these fatuous definitions, they cannot be taken seriously.

McPharlin, whose etymology we followed, defines the puppet as "a theatrical figure moved under human control" (1949: 1). Bil Baird, one of the most influential producers of twentieth-century American puppetry, defines the puppet as "an inanimate figure made to move by human effort before an audience" (1965: 13). The majority of definitions given by scholars and practitioners of puppetry merely restate the elements that are explicit or implicit in these definitions; let us work with them.

These definitions are obviously superior to those offered by etymology or dictionaries. They correctly observe the puppet as theatrical and as existing before an audience, thus making a fundamental distinction between the puppet that performs and the doll with which a solitary child might play. Such a doll may indeed be used as a puppet, but it seems obvious that not all dolls are puppets, and, conversely, that not all puppets are dolls. The definitions also correctly observe the puppet as being "under human control" and "moved by human effort," thus making a fundamental distinction between the puppet, which is responsive to immediate and variable control, and the automaton, which is motivated via some mechanical or electronic device to perform, unresponsively, a limited series of actions. Again, such an automaton may be used as a puppet, but it seems obvious that not all automata are puppets, and, conversely, that not all puppets are automata. Finally, the broadness of these definitions allows for the vast scope of activity that people are talking about when they talk about puppets.

Notwithstanding these strengths, McPharlin's and Baird's definitions suffer from three serious problems. The first problem exists despite the broadness of the definitions, and arises from a failure to consider fully the possibilities inherent in the puppet's sign-system of design. McPharlin writes that the puppet is a "theatrical figure," but throughout his work (see McPharlin 1938 and 1949) he takes for granted what Baird makes plain: that the figure of the puppet is inanimate. But need the puppet, in fact, be inanimate?

Some examples will be useful. Let us take, for instance, the theatrical figure of a baby, brought on-stage by a living "father" who obviously operates him, and who sings to him a lullaby; the baby looks around at the audience, plays with the father, and so on. His head is carved wood, and his body a cloth sack. When he rolls over to sleep, he exposes a naked behind, which is nothing other than the back of the operator's hand (Obraztsov 1985 [1981]: 84–87).

And let us take the figure of a drunkard, who sings a lyric of drunken sorrow, all the while pouring himself one glass of vodka after another. His head is stuffed cloth, with a mouth that opens and closes; his body is little more than a shirt that hangs from hidden wooden shoulders. The hand that does the pouring, however, connected to the body by a sleeve, is the actual hand of his operator (Obraztsov 1985 [1981]: 115–17). Neither of the theatrical figures in these examples is entirely inanimate, as both of them incorporate and expose living flesh; yet few people would deny that they are puppets. The possibilities inherent in the puppet's sign-system of design are not exhausted by figures that are entirely inanimate.

More extreme examples can be presented. Let us take, for instance, the theatrical figures of two lovers. To the accompaniment of Tchaikovsky's "We Were Sitting Alone by a Murmuring Brook," the lovers meet one last time; they approach one another, laugh and cry, sigh with regret, hug and kiss, and finally part. Their heads are little more than small spheres of wood, while their bodies are nothing other than the two bare hands of their operator. The wooden spheres are affixed to one finger of each hand (Obraztsov 1985 [1981]: 107–108).

And let us take the figures of two combatants: without a word spoken, they argue and fight, and one is subdued while the other is triumphant. But the figures are nothing other than living human hands. The triumphant hand becomes a wall; the subdued hand makes a fist and knocks against it; the wall will not give, and the subdued hand falls away; the triumphant hand makes a fist; both hands spread out, open-palmed, in a gesture that silently asks "Why?"

There is little or nothing inanimate about the figures of these two examples: living hands dominate the performances. And still, the hands, as used here, are generally taken to be puppets, for they are not only perceived by the audience as pairs of hands in themselves, but also as something other than hands. The possibilities inherent in the puppet's sign-system of design encompass figures that are not predominantly inanimate, and even figures that are not at all inanimate.

The last of these examples is a sketch about the Berlin Wall, presented by Burr Tillstrom to the 1980 International Puppetry Convention; the three previous examples are sketches by Obraztsov, who writes:

> The principle of [the hand-puppet] consists of two elements only: the human hand and a puppet's head. [The puppet's body] is only a costume. But strip a hand puppet of its costume and leave your hand exposed with the puppet's head on your finger and the puppet remains a puppet. (1950: 186)

In fact, as we have seen, one may go so far as to strip the puppet of its head, and the human hand can still remain a puppet. But if this is so, and the design possibilities of the puppet go so far as to abjure any use of the inanimate, then how are we to allow for the actor as puppet, while maintaining the distinction between actor and puppet?

Obraztsov makes a telling remark concerning his sketch with the figure of the baby: "My right hand, on which I wear the puppet, lives apart from me with a rhythm and a character of its own. . . . [It] conducts a silent dialogue with me or, ignoring me altogether, lives its independent life" (1950: 155). This "living apart" of the puppet, with "a character of its own," is a vital point. It seems apparent that when an audience sees the back of the operator's hand as the baby's behind, it perceives the hand not only as a hand, but, more important, as part of the figure of the baby. Similarly, when an audience sees the operator's hand as the puppet character's hand, it is perceived not only as a living hand, but, more important, as the hand of the figure. In each case, the hand that wears the puppet "lives apart," and is perceived apart, from the actor, and partakes, in the perception of the audience, of the same nature as the rest of the figure. That is, it is perceived not so much as a hand, as it is an object.

This principle extends to the hands that Obraztsov uses as puppets' bodies, and to the hands that Tillstrom uses to signify bodies, a wall, and the ideas of anger, supremacy, and mental anguish. Because of the manner in which the hand is employed in the design of these puppets, even if, as with Tillstrom, it is the sole element of design, and because of the manner in which the puppet is given movement or speech, the hand of the actor is perceived to be "apart" from the actor. Thus, the actor may be called a puppet when the actor presents him or herself in such a way that the audience perceives him or her, not only as alive, but also, in whole or in part, as an object.

A corollary question arises: how are we to distinguish between the actor who is perceived as an object and the actor who merely performs in mask or costume? To give a simple example, is the Mickey Mouse who greets visitors at Disneyland to be considered a puppet?

This question is made especially difficult to answer by the desire of many people involved with the puppet to annex the mask into the field of puppetry. Baird writes:

> Masks . . . are just an evolutionary step or two away from the puppet. When a single masked dancer began to appear as a performer . . . it was the beginning of theatrical performance and a stepping-off place for the mask to become a puppet. Gradually . . . the mask moved upward, off the head, and was held in front of the body. Later, it moved farther away and was made to live by . . . manipulation. (1965: 30)

The anthropological basis for Baird's assertion is, of course, debatable, but clearly he believes there to be an intimate relationship between the actor in mask or costume and the puppet.

Peter Arnott, the late British performer and scholar who presented the classical repertoire with puppets, would go even beyond such intimacy: "We may say . . . that whenever an actor dons a mask—either literally, as in Greek and Roman plays, or figuratively, as when he plays a strongly typed part—he is abnegating his individuality and making of himself a puppet" (1964: 77). Annexation such as this certainly goes too far, as it would turn a goodly portion of what is universally presumed to be live theatre into puppetry. The definition of the puppet can scarcely be stretched to this extent without snapping altogether, severing the word from any particular meaning.

To distinguish between the actor subsumed in the puppet and the actor wearing a mask or costume, we must consider the perception of the audience: if the audience perceives the mask or costume to be nothing more than an object of dress worn by a living actor, then that is all it is; but if the audience perceives the actor in the mask or costume to be but a part of the object, then it must be recognized as a puppet. Our Mickey Mouse, with his patently human structural physiognomy, is surely not perceived as an object, and so is not a puppet, but simply an actor in costume.

The first problem with McPharlin's and Baird's definitions, then, can be solved with the realization that the possibilities inherent in the puppet's sign-system of design transcend the inanimate. The puppet is an "object" only in the perception of the audience. It will be useful, when not explicitly noting the perception of the audience, to employ the quotation marks, reminding us that the word is not limited to the inanimate, but, rather, implicitly refers to the audience's perception of the figure in question.

If this first problem with the definitions exists despite their broadness, the second problem exists because of that broadness. In trying to open up the concept of what should be called a puppet, they open it up too far. When McPharlin writes that the puppet is "moved under human control," and Baird that it is "made to move by human effort," they suggest that any theatrical figure so moved is a puppet. But is this true?

Let us take a mundane theatrical example: a cane rests against a scenic flat bearing the representation of a window; at some point, stagehands move the cane and the flat to new locations. The cane and the flat are certainly "theatrical figures" and "inanimate figures"; they certainly have been "moved under human control," or "made to move by human effort." Yet it could scarcely be imagined that anyone would want to call them puppets. It is, of course, perfectly possible to use canes and flats as puppets; it is possible, it may well be argued, to use anything as a puppet. But clearly, this cane and this flat are not puppets. Somehow, the puppet must be distinguished from props and scenery, for not every object given movement on the stage can be considered a puppet.

A solution to this problem is vaguely implied by McPharlin's use of the word theatrical, which should probably be taken to suggest something of a more significant nature than props and scenery. Marjorie Batchelder, a major force in American puppetry both as a scholar and a producer, does not settle for mere suggestion: "the puppet is an actor participating in some kind of theatrical performance" (1947: xv). This is to the point, as neither the cane nor the flat can be construed to be acting, although both partake, in their separate ways, of theatrical representation. But Batchelder's solution, although not an attempt to annex live acting into puppetry, poses a semantic problem: the puppet is certainly an actor of some sort, but as we have seen, it must somehow be distinguished from the living actor if the word is to retain any meaning. Batchelder makes this distinction by referring to the puppet's "mechanical means" of motivation (1947: xv). This, however, is also problematic: hand-puppets, as well as hands used as puppets, are given motivation without any mechanical means; what is more, the semantic confusion between puppet and actor lingers despite the distinction. To avoid this confusion, it will be useful to examine precisely how the puppet can be construed to act.

Look again at Baird's use of the word inanimate. Such a word compels consideration not only of itself, but also of its opposite. Obraztsov writes about "the process by which the inanimate becomes animate" (1967 [1965]: 19). If the puppet is inanimate, then its theatrical significance is not created by its being moved, as such, but by its being animated. Neither the cane nor the flat in the example just offered can be construed to have been animated. This solution, however, although quite common, poses semantic difficulties of its own.

To begin with a minor difficulty: the word animation has been taken over to a large degree by the film industry, with its animation of cartoon figures. Although there are significant similarities between cartoon animation and puppetry, and although certain styles of puppetry, such as "Claymation," can be created only with the techniques of cartoon animation, we should not gloss over the even more significant differences between the two media by employing the same word in discussion of them.

The major difficulty is that to animate something means, in the root sense of the word, to give it the breath of life. As a metaphor, this has great resonance for puppetry. But non-metaphorically, it is absurd, for, of course, the puppet does not actually live. As Obraztsov admits:

In reality, no inanimate object can be animated—not a brick, rag, toy (even if it is mechanical), or theatrical puppet—no matter how expertly it moves when manipulated by a puppeteer. Regardless of circumstances, the objects listed above remain objects lacking any biological features. However, in man's hands any object—the same brick, rag, sole of a shoe, or bottle—can fulfill the function of a living object in man's associative fantasy. It can move, laugh, cry, or declare its love. (1985 [1981]: 264)

Animation, as such, is not really at issue with the puppet; rather, at issue is the movement of an object in such a manner that it can, in Obraztsov's terms, "fulfill the function of a living object in man's associative fantasy," or, in the terms of this study, be imagined to have life. Thus, although props and scenery may be given movement on the stage, the movement given to the puppet is of a sort that encourages the imagination of life.

Another corollary question arises: is the puppet a puppet when it is given no movement, but sits at rest in some closet or museum? We honor various objects at rest with the title puppet, but on what authority? Michael R. Malkin, an American scholar and producer, reports that "African puppets often bear little relationship to Western concepts of how puppets should look, [and so] clear, unequivocal identification of many figures [as puppets] is often difficult to obtain" (1977: 71).

The implications of this are of great importance. It is only as a result of familiarity with particular traditions of puppetry that we are able to identify certain objects, or, more generally, certain classes of objects, as puppets. Thus, we in the West are aware of certain classes of objects that we know to be dedicated especially to usage as puppets, such as hand-puppets and marionettes, and can easily call any object a puppet that seems to belong to such a class. But a vast variety of objects, belonging to classes of objects not dedicated especially to puppetry, such as human hands, wooden spheres, kitchen utensils, and so on, have, in fact, been used as puppets. It follows that accordance of the title puppet upon any object at rest, or, more properly, not in performance, can only be tentative. The puppet cannot be defined simply in terms of design. Rather, it must be defined as something other than an object or a class of objects characterized by particular physical form; it must be defined, that is, with reference to the additional sign-systems that help the audience imagine it to have life.

Malkin himself understands this. As he writes in a different article, "the animated object becomes a puppet not when the operator assumes complete control of it, but at the infinitely more subtle moment when the object seems to develop a life force of its own" (1980: 9).

The second problem, then, can be solved by the realization that the movement of a stage figure does not necessarily invoke, nor intend to invoke, the audience's imagination that it possesses "life." Indeed, it will be useful, when not explicitly noting the imagination of the audience, to employ the quotation marks, reminding the reader that the word does not refer to any real life in the puppet, but, rather, implicitly refers to the audience's willful imagination when viewing the figure in question.

The third problem with the definitions of McPharlin and Baird is their suggestion that movement is the defining characteristic of the puppet. McPharlin states categorically that "it is movement, actual or illusory, which gives a puppet animation" (1938: 81). Movement is, of course, one of the three sign-systems whose signs constitute the puppet; and, following McPharlin, it might well be the most significant of the sign-systems. As Louis Duranty, a nineteenth-century Frenchman, writes, "what the puppets do entirely dominates what they say" (quoted in Veltruský 1983: 97).

On the other hand, the puppet in performance can remain motionless for extended periods of time, and can, on rare occasions, remain without actual motion for the duration of its performance, and yet be something other than a mere figure of design—that is, something other than a statue. This is because the sign-system of speech is also available to the puppet, and in the absence of puppet movement, the possibilities inherent in this sign-system, in conjunction with those of design, can allow the audience to imagine the puppet as having life. The sign-systems of design and speech are of vital importance to puppetry, and in overlooking them, the definitions of McPharlin and Baird overlook constitutive aspects of the puppet.

Henryk Jurkowski, whose doubts about the synchronic approach were discussed in the introduction, offers a definition of the puppet theatre that incorporates all three sign-systems available to the puppet:

> The puppet theatre is a theatre art, the main and basic feature differentiating it from the live theatre being the fact that the speaking and performing object makes temporal use of the physical sources of the vocal and motor powers, which are present outside the object. The relations between the object (the puppet) and the power sources [the speakers and/or manipulators] change all the time and their variations are of great semiological and aesthetical significance. (1988 [1983]: 79–80)

One should note that this is a definition of the puppet theatre, and not of the puppet itself. Yet surely we can see the essentials of a puppet definition here: the puppet is an object given "temporal use" of external "vocal and motor powers," the externality of which is of decisive importance.

In giving this definition, Jurkowski appears to be making just the sort of synchronic statement he previously disparaged. Be that as it may, his definition would be an advance over McPharlin's and Baird's if only because of its recognition of each of the three sign-systems. But it goes further. Its insistence on the importance of the separation of and relationship between the object and its "power sources" prepares the way for analysis of how the sign-systems operate independently and corporately. There are, however, three problems with Jurkowski's definition as well.

The first problem is that while the definition recognizes the three separate sign-systems, it seems to contend that both speech and movement must be present if we are to construe an object to be a puppet: Jurkowski refers to "the speaking *and* performing object," "the physical sources of the vocal *and* motor powers" (italics added). Moreover, contrary to McPharlin's categorical assertion about movement, Jurkowski goes on to be categorical about speech. Charles Magnin, a nineteenth-century French historian of the theatre, argues that "the separation of word and action is precisely that which constitutes the puppet play" (quoted in Proschan 1983: 20). Jurkowski refines this argument: "The separability of the speaking object and the physical source of the word

. . . is the distinctive feature of the puppet theatre" (1988 [1983]: 79).

But consider two cases: in the first, a narrative dance is presented by inanimate figures that are given movement on-stage to the accompaniment of music; in the second, a narrative dance is presented on-stage by live dancers, to the accompaniment of character voices. In the first case, despite the absence of any given speech, the figures on-stage could scarcely be thought of as anything but puppets; in the second case, despite the presence of a separate source of speech, the live dancers could scarcely be thought of as anything but live dancers. Jurkowski's insistence that the sign-systems of speech and movement operate always in tandem leads to a denial of what is obviously a puppet. By refining Magnin's argument with the assertion that the separation is between speech and object, rather than speech and action, Jurkowski avoids total absurdity; but his insistence on the primacy of speech over movement still tends in that direction. The problem of the relations between the two sign-systems can, however, be easily solved, by emphasizing neither of the two sign-systems over the other, a priori, but rather by allowing their signs to exist separately or together, in conjunction with the designed object itself, in the constitution of the puppet.

The second problem with Jurkowski's definition is that when he speaks of the puppet as an object, he means precisely that: something of a wholly inanimate nature. As such, puppetry cannot incorporate any part of the live actor in the puppet. In fact, as we will see later, Jurkowski would go so far as to consider disallowing the hand-puppet as a puppet, because the audience focuses on the mime of the puppet-operator's hand, on which the puppet itself is but a costume (1988 [1979]: 21–22). Thus, Jurkowski severely limits the possibilities inherent in the puppet's sign-system of design; what is more, he defies the general understanding of what is meant by the word puppet. This problem, as we have seen, can be resolved by taking seriously the perception of the audience: what is perceived to be an object, regardless of its true nature, can indeed be a puppet.

The third problem with Jurkowski's definition is that while it accounts for the puppet's three sign-systems, it does not refer to the purpose of the deployment of the puppet's signs: to create something that an audience will imagine to have life. Jurkowski is not unaware of this purpose, for he writes of the puppet "as both puppet and scenic character" (1988 [1983]: 78). But this awareness is not to be found in his definition. This problem can be solved with the simple acknowledgment of the desired theatrical result: the imagination of life for the puppet that occurs when its signs are competently deployed.

It should be noted that Jurkowski has recently expressed misgivings about his definition: "I doubt the possibility of producing a universal, coherent definition of modern puppet theatre. . . . I guess that we will have to study each genre of the so-called puppet theatre in order to define its characteristics and its language" (1990: 18). This doubt arises from the development of what Jurkowski calls "the theatre of the puppet *in the broadest sense*," in which the puppet "has a profane [rather than sacred] nature and structure," and in which "the performer does not serve the puppet anymore; he makes the puppet serve him and his ideas" (1990: 17). Given his deep concern with the matter of "service," of which we will see more, Jurkowski cannot help but believe that productions in which the performance of the operator is of equal or greater significance than the performance of the puppet must partake of a different nature than that of conventional puppet theatre. Nonetheless, the core definition of the puppet that we have discerned in Jurkowski's definition of puppet theatre seems unaffected by this development in modern puppetry, and remains with the strengths and weaknesses we have discussed.

Before setting forth the basis for a new definition of the puppet, let us briefly summarize the foregoing analysis. It will be recalled that the first problem with the definitions of McPharlin and Baird is that, despite their broadness, they do not allow for the actor as puppet, failing to do justice to the possibilities inherent in the sign-system of design. This problem is resolved with the realization that the living actor can present him or herself, in part or in whole, in such a way that the audience perceives the actor just as it perceives the rest of the figure: as an object.

The second problem with these definitions is that, in their broadness, they fail to distinguish between the puppet and scenery or props, because they ignore the animating purpose of puppet movement. This problem is resolved with the realization that the puppet is given movement for the explicit purpose of encouraging the audience to imagine that the puppet has something that, in fact, it does not have: its own life.

The third problem with these definitions is that, with their emphasis on movement, they overlook the importance of the puppet's sign-systems of design, and especially, speech. This problem is resolved with the realization that design and speech are, indeed, two of the three basic sign-systems of the puppet.

Jurkowski's definition solves this third problem, but gives it a new twist by contending that the sign-systems of movement and speech must be used in tandem, and that of the two, the sign-system of speech is the more significant. Further, this definition insists that the puppet must be a pure object, not incorporating any part of the living actor. Finally, this definition fails to acknowledge the theatrical effect of the puppet. But as we have seen, these problems can also be resolved.

Taking all of our solutions together, the way is at last clear to answer the question that was posed at the start of this chapter: when people talk about puppets, they are talking about figures perceived by an audience to be objects that are given design, movement, and frequently, speech, in such a way that the audience imagines them to have life.

The formulation of this answer is just the starting point for a full theoretical comprehension of the puppet. Before such a comprehension can be developed, it will be necessary to explore the nature of the puppet's ubiquitous appeal; to explore, that is, the various explanations that have been put forward for the survival of the puppet. Such an exploration will, ultimately, lead us to an expansion of the basic definition just offered, for the problem of explanation is, as we will see, profoundly related to that of definition. Only when we have discovered the basis of the puppet's continuing theatrical existence will we be able to comprehend the particular aesthetic nature of the puppet as perceived object and imagined life.

2

STANDARD EXPLANATIONS

We have explored what people are talking about when they talk about puppets; but why is it that the puppet exists to be talked about at all? Batchelder sets out the problem: "One is led to wonder what qualities inherent in the puppet theatre have given it sufficient vitality to maintain itself as an independent art, and what fundamental appeal it contains which has insured its popularity among so many different kinds of people" (1947: 278). The burden of explanation is to demonstrate what these qualities are, or even to demonstrate that a single quality is involved in all puppetry. There can be no doubt that the puppet theatre has any number of particular qualities. But is there any explanation of its endurance and appeal that depends upon a quality that might prove to be constant, existing beside or beneath all others?

Previous writers have proposed solutions to this problem, but these solutions have rarely been reviewed systematically, and so the relationships between them are not clearly established. The following review will consider the proposed solutions in three sections, each focusing on one of the major components of a puppet production: the artist, the puppet, and the audience. It should be noted that some writers have proposed solutions that cross over the somewhat arbitrary borders of these groupings, and that the purpose of this review is not so much to categorize possible solutions as it is to find a coherent way of bringing them to light.

EXPLANATIONS BASED UPON THE ARTIST

There can be no question that puppetry offers a distinctive array of possibilities to the theatrical artist. These possibilities are of three basic types: first, the puppet theatre offers the artist a remarkable opportunity for control over a medium; second, it offers the artist the puppet's license to act and speak with remarkable freedom from restraint; third, it offers the artist a medium that is, by its very nature, unbounded by reality.

In puppetry, the artist can, and frequently does, perform every task necessary to the production of a play. David Currell, a British puppet-artist, boasts that "the puppeteer is . . . a unique combination of sculptor, modeller, painter, needleworker, electrician, carpenter, actor, writer, producer, designer, and inventor" (1987 [1985]: 1).

It should be noted that the very use of the word puppeteer seems to imply this notion of a single, all-controlling artist. The word itself was coined early this century by the founder of the Chicago Little Theatre Marionettes, Ellen Van Volkenburg. Louise Martin tells us that "they did not know what to call the manipulator-actor back in that day," and that Van Volkenburg, with some misgivings, hit on the word puppeteer following from the term for a mule-driver, a muleteer (1945: 5). A goodly portion of contemporary American puppetry traces its roots, directly or indirectly, to the Chicago Little Theatre Marionettes, and part of their heritage has been the word puppeteer. The word is certainly more tractable than locutions such as puppet-designer, puppet-operator, puppet-speaker, and so on. And given that, as Currell notes, these roles, and yet others, are often performed by a single person, the rise of the puppeteer has probably been inevitable. Indeed, the worthy organization that aspires to advance the art of puppetry in the United States calls itself the Puppeteers of America.

Nonetheless, the word harbors the presumption of the all-controlling artist. If, as in our Japanese example, certain people design and create the head, the wig, and the costume of the puppet, while others operate the assembled figure on-stage, while yet others provide its speech, does not the term puppeteer seem misleading? Erik Kolár, a Czech scholar, speaks of the puppeteer as being in "inseparable unity with his puppet" (1967 [1965]: 32). But in our Japanese example, there are two or three operators, and the puppet might be transferred to the control of yet other operators. Can we truly speak of an inseparable union between the puppet and any one of these operators, not to mention the various designers and, especially, the speakers, who also make vital contributions to the presentation of the puppet; can we speak, with much significance at all, of a puppeteer in Currell's sense of the word? In light of these difficulties, this study eschews usage of the word puppeteer, in favor of more precise terms when necessary, and of puppet-artist when a general, but less loaded, term is required.

The puppet-artist, especially in the guise of puppeteer, can be assured that collaborators will not impose on his or her singular artistic vision by dispensing with the need for any collaboration. Arnott contends that "the besetting problem of those who would create a work of art in the theatre is unity. . . . It follows that . . . unity is easiest to achieve when only one creative mind is involved" (1964: 74). And, as Batchelder notes, puppetry offers the theatrical artist the best chance to attain such unity, in that "the puppet show is usually built on a smaller scale than a play for human theatre, hence synthesis is more easily attained" (1947: 280).

When artists speak of a problem in attaining unity or synthesis in artistic expression, they suggest that collaboration is generally more of a hindrance than a help. The collaboration most resented is that which takes place with actors. Arthur Symons, a turn-of-the-century American writer on the theatre, complained that "the living actor, even when he condescends to subordinate himself to the requirements of pantomime, has always what he is proud to call his temperament; in other words so much personal caprice" (1909: 3). Symons was a significant influence on Edward Gordon Craig, the British theatre visionary, who took this line of reasoning to its logical, if highly rhetorical, extreme: "The actor must go, and in his place comes the inanimate figure—the Übermarionette we may call him" (1911: 81).

Craig would have absolute control over every aspect of his theatre; and though he would have others operate, or even be, his "Übermarionettes," his control, nonetheless, would be undiminished. As Irene Eynat-Confino points out:

In the "Über-Marions" notebooks Craig gives several reasons for inventing the Übermarionette. . . . [Among them is the desire to] eliminate the element of chance in acting. . . . Since Craig intended to provide carefully worked out plans for all movements . . . the human failings of the [operators or actors] were of no consequence. (1987: 89)

It is perhaps worth noting that Craig never actually produced any shows of this Übermarionette Theatre. At least one reason for this, beyond the usual financial difficulties that beset Craig, is plain: the extreme difficulty of any one person maintaining absolute control over a substantial theatrical venture. Indeed, Batchelder remarks on the generally desirable "small scale" of puppetry; also, the productions of Peter Arnott were one-man shows.

Many puppet-artists, following Craig, aspire to create a unified, synthetic art through the exertion of an absolute control approximating that of the painter or sculptor. But it seems a strange assumption that the finest art exists only as the expression of the solitary artist. Collaboration in the theatre has certainly produced great art — greater, it would seem, than any solitary theatre artist has yet produced. And such art has attained unity and synthesis despite, or even because of, the various egos and visions of the collaborators. It could, indeed, be argued that these egos and visions, along with the talents that accompany them, have a symbiotic effect on one other, resulting in a work far greater than any one of them is capable of achieving.

More significantly, absolute artistic control is not a general characteristic of the puppet theatre. Among the examples given in the introduction, the British "Punch and Judy" show was a one-man performance, and that performer, Percy Press, Jr., was responsible for every aspect involved, even if some of those aspects were traditional, and merely required his mediation. But all of the other examples were collaborative efforts. The Japanese performance involved the largest number of artists: two or three operators for each puppet, with as many as three puppets on-stage at one time; at least one musician and sometimes three or four, on-stage and off; at least one narrator, and sometimes three or four, on-stage and off; and backstage, any number of costumers, head-carvers, wig-makers, prop-builders, and so on (Adachi 1985: 9–11).

Neither is absolute artistic control a unique characteristic of the puppet theatre. Any live one-man show offers the artist the same level of control as is offered by the one-man puppet show. For example, Hal Holbrook's production of *Mark Twain Tonight* is as self-contained as any puppet production might be. It should also be noted that the opportunity for control that puppetry offers the artist is frequently taken up less for artistic reasons than for financial ones, at least in America. Given the economic realities for puppet productions, it is often only by working alone that an artist can earn a living; collaboration risks financial ruin.

The opportunity for control, then, is not an opportunity invariably taken up in the puppet theatre, and it is not an opportunity unique to the puppet theatre. As valuable as it can be, both artistically and economically, and as frequently as it is employed, it is not a single quality that can explain the enduring appeal of the puppet.

The puppet theatre also offers an artist the puppet's license to act and speak with remarkable freedom. The puppet, not being a living person, cannot be held responsible for its actions and words; yet these actions and words are not directly those of the puppet-artist, and so neither does he or she seem to bear responsibility for them. Thus, the puppet is especially suited to the flaunting of social conventions and consequences. Two examples will demonstrate the degree to which this license is taken.

Bart P. Roccoberton, Jr., director of the Puppetry Program at the University of Connecticut, Storrs, tells a story of his visit to the home of a famous American puppet-artist. The visit was to include a viewing of the artist's collection of puppets, and then a dinner. Upon his arrival, Roccoberton was greeted by the artist's most famous puppet. It was this puppet, operated, of course, by the artist, that guided him along through the collection, while the artist, in his own voice, offered only a few stray comments. When dinnertime neared, Roccoberton witnessed an argument between the artist and his puppet: the artist suggested they all have a drink and then dine, while the puppet insisted on a need for rest, wishing the wearisome visitor to leave. Roccoberton was astonished to hear the artist reluctantly agree with the puppet; shortly thereafter he was shown to the door, with the artist apologizing for the puppet's moodiness (Roccoberton 1982).

Bogatyrev reports on a similar sense of license: "A certain puppeteer was subpoenaed, accused of making political attacks from a puppet stage. The puppeteer appeared in court carrying the puppet Kašpárek and announced that it was not his fault, but Kašpárek's" (1983 [1973]: 54). Unfortunately, we do not learn whether the puppeteer's explanation was accepted by the court.

These examples are, of course, extreme, but the puppet in performance retains an extraordinary freedom. Recall our consideration of "Punch and Judy": Punch commits a series of violent murders, all to the glee of his audience. George Speaight, in his masterful study *The History of the English Puppet Theatre*, traces Punch's lineage and concludes:

> Approached historically . . . Punch will not be seen as an inhuman monster who goes through life striking and murdering everyone who crosses his path, but as the old comedian . . . who only murders each new character brought before him as the quickest way of ending *that* scene and getting on with the next. Perhaps that is the fundamental reason we laugh at Punch, and are not horrified. . . . We have sensed . . . that behind his wooden victories there lies the arch-type of "he who gets slapped," the primitive and eternal clown. (1990 [1955]: 184–85)

No doubt that Punch is a puppet version of the archetypical clown. Yet this does not seem sufficient explanation for a comedy that contains such ceaseless brutality. One need only imagine a similar performance by live actors: would it not be insupportable? In fact, so much wanton killing is rarely, if ever, presented in live theatre comedy.

The puppet, however, being nothing more than a theatrical "object," cannot be construed as having the "living" responsibility even of the actor, and so the successive murders of a dozen or so characters become a cause for laughter, and not concern. It should also be noted that the license of the puppet on-stage is not limited to physical action. As McPharlin points out, "Certainly Punch may go further without offense in making quips upon delicate subjects, than could a living actor" (1938: 16).

The license of the puppet is most often exhibited in the performance of satire and parody, and is predicated on the realization that because the puppet is not a living person, it is free to present a corrosive portrait of those who are. Arnott, in a comment on Obraztsov's work, observes that "it is in the field of satire that the puppet theatre seems to have established its widest adult appeal. Puppets lend themselves obviously and easily to caricature" (1964: 50).

Obraztsov himself makes a distinction between three different kinds of satire or parody at which the puppet is especially adept: the " 'portrait' parody . . . [a] parody of a definite character, [in which] pure imitation [of some feature or behavior] is the kernel of the portrait"; the " 'generalized' parody . . . [a parody of] a group of people who have common professional, social, or other distinguishing features," in which it is those group features that are caricatured; and the kind of parody that "consists in parodying a given subject . . . or rather, theme," which might be called thematic satire (1950: 164–65).

Portrait parody works in a simple manner that need not be detailed; we should note only that its success depends on the audience's familiarity with the person being parodied. Generalized parody is well illustrated by an example given by Obraztsov:

> There are some opera and concert singers . . . for whom the performance is only a pretext for displaying their talents. . . . They consider it necessary to display their breathing, so they drag their *fermata* for half a minute. . . . I wanted to make fun of a singer of that sort. Of his "magnificent" voice, his "immense" temperament, of his swaggering walk, his hands clutching the crumpled music . . . and the exaggerated stretch of the neck for the "brilliant" high notes. (1950: 167)

Obraztsov constructed a puppet of such a singer: it came on-stage full of pompous self-glory, indulged in every mannerism appropriate to that glory in the course of a song, and consummated the song on a note so high and long that the puppet's neck stretched four times its original length (1950: 167–68). Obraztsov also gives examples of thematic satires he has created, but they need not be detailed; the Nigerian performance described earlier will serve as example. In addition to its portrait parodies of tribal members, it presented a broad satire on the themes of tribal life and governance (Messenger 1971: 208).

Clearly, then, the puppet offers the artist a highly effective means of indulging in satire or parody. The puppet is especially capable of pointing out the foibles, on every level, of humankind. The significance of this is borne out in the experience of everyone who works in the puppet theatre in America: satire and parody are the basic staples of puppetry as it is presented here for adults.

And of course, satire and parody are not limited to puppet theatre for adults; "Punch and Judy" contains many elements of parody. Is not Judy a generalized parody of the shrewish wife? Punch also has disputes with a policeman and a hangman; are not these characters also generalized parodies of familiar types?

Despite the widespread reliance on the license of the puppet for satire and parody, such license is not a significant factor in all puppet performance. The Javanese performance described in the introduction, for example, did not depend on it except for occasional comic relief: the puppet's license had little bearing on the dramatic presentation of mythical history. Indeed, it would seem that most traditional performances concerned with mythological presentation have scant interest in exploiting the puppet's license, dedicated as they are to presenting tales of gods and heroes.

While the live theatre does not have recourse to the broader license of the puppet, there is theatrical license enough to allow for actions and speech that would not be condoned outside the theatre. One need only imagine what the reaction of the public would be to a real-life Macbeth, or to the nudity and vulgarity, or even the near-treason and blasphemy, that one accepts as a matter of course in the theatre. And, of course, live theatre productions of such plays as Jonson's *Every Man in His Humour* and Caryl Churchill's *Serious Money*, as well as the work of innumerable comic impersonators, remind us that the live theatre has ample ability to partake of satire and parody.

The puppet also offers an artist a medium that is unbounded by nature, predicated on the realization that because the puppet is nothing more than a theatrical figure, a cipher, it can be made to present beings of every imaginable type, with each type partaking of the same theatrical "reality" as any other.

Batchelder writes that "the enduring success of the puppet theatre rests . . . upon the facility with which it brings into juxtaposition the real and the imaginary, endowing both with equal plausibility" (1947: 292). Malkin argues, developing the same idea:

> Puppetry has played a vital role in the development of what can be called the dramatic concept of the *plausible impossible*. . . . [This] is the link between the world of the real and the realm of pure fantasy. . . . It is in this sense that puppetry represents a basic theatrical concept; it represents dramatic imagination in one of its most fluid forms. (1975: 6–7)

The significance of the "plausible impossible" is borne out in the experience of everyone who currently works in American puppet theatre: fantasy and folklore, replete with impossible characters, are the basic staples of puppetry as it is presented here in children's theatre.

Of course, the "plausible impossible" is not limited to puppet theatre for children. Recall our Indian and American examples given earlier: in the former, the figure of a girl was transformed into that of an ogre; in the latter, numbers themselves were given "life." Throughout the world, puppet-artists performing for children and adults alike take advantage of the puppet's ability to mingle the worlds of reality and fantasy.

Despite widespread reliance on the plausible impossible, however, the commingling of reality and fantasy is not a factor in all puppet performance. Our Nigerian example did not rely on it to any great degree, for the aptitude to present the impossible plausibly is not necessary for the presentation of social satire. Indeed, it would seem that most traditional performances concerned with parody and satire forego intermixing the two worlds, preferring to explore in depth only the world of the real.

While the live theatre cannot integrate the real and the fantastic with the innate ease of puppetry, it can convincingly present integrated worlds: productions of such works as Shakespeare's *A Midsummer Night's Dream* and James Barrie's *Peter Pan* demonstrate not only that the live theatre can challenge puppetry in this regard, but that the live theatre can offer dimensions unavailable to puppetry. Does not a live

Peter Pan in flight evoke a greater sense of wonder and amazement than can a marionette?

In that the puppet offers its particular license, on the one hand, and its aptitude for the plausible impossible, on the other, it seems clear that neither quality can, in itself, be the one that accounts for the puppet's widespread endurance. Indeed, as we have seen, traditional performances that rely on one tend not to need the other. But still, these qualities have a certain commonality, predicated as they are on the puppet being not a living person, but only a theatrical figure. As this is the case, we must next consider the manner in which the puppet is enabled to create theatrical performance.

EXPLANATIONS BASED UPON THE PUPPET

It is axiomatic that theatrical performance involves representation, or one might say make-believe play, of one sort or another. The puppet is made to represent a character, as we have seen in the introduction, through the deployment of signs chosen from its constitutive sign-systems of design, movement, and speech. Can the widespread and enduring appeal of the puppet be explained by its particular manner of deploying signs to represent that which it is not?

Batchelder, as noted earlier, contends that puppetry endures because of its "facility [for the] juxtaposition [of] the real and the imaginary." This facility, she suggests, arises from the fact that "direct characterization is the puppet actor's strongest quality. There is no pretense. A puppet *is* the character it portrays; it is not a human being dressed up and pretending to be that character" (1947: 288). This ability to characterize directly, Batchelder contends, allows for the juxtaposition of real and imaginary elements, as both are presented to the audience without the interfering pretense of live actors.

Batchelder's contention that the puppet offers no pretense, however, is untenable, for the puppet is certainly engaged in pretense, albeit a different pretense than that of the live actor. The actor pretends to be some*one* other than he or she is; the puppet pretends to be some*thing* other than it is, by pretending to have life. Such pretense is fundamental to all puppetry, and cannot be overlooked. Contrary to Batchelder, then, an explanation of the puppet must account for how the puppet is capable of the pretense of life.

It is commonplace to observe that puppetry has traditionally achieved such a pretense by re-creating live theatre, which itself "imitates" life. McPharlin writes:

> The history of the puppet theatre, until its revival as an independent art, was a course of imitation of the larger theatre. It took over Punch when he was nearly played out on the stage. It presented medieval moralities far into the Renaissance. It celebrated naval engagements and sieges until they had become legendary. It perpetuated dances and vaudeville turns when they were hoary. This made it a minor and reflective branch of the theatre. (1949: 395)

The historical rationale for this small-scale re-creation of live theatre, this taking over of "played out" aspects, is simple: live theatre, being of greater scale and expense, could regularly be mounted only in certain urban centers; the puppet theatre, which could travel easily — in many cases, on a single man's back — could re-create and reproduce it endlessly in the rural hinterlands. The sense that puppetry is a derivative, rather than an original, form of theatre derives from this history.

The revival to which McPharlin refers took place around the turn of the century, and may be characterized precisely as an affirmation of puppetry as an original, rather than derivative, form of theatre. In Jurkowski's terms, the puppet developed its own theatrical "sign system" (1988 [1983]: 76).

The history that McPharlin recites is affirmed by Jan Malík of Czechoslovakia, who has served as secretary-general of UNIMA: "For many centuries . . . the puppet theatre . . . represented a kind of miniature edition of the live theatre. . . . Indeed, to this day we find among marionette operators a tendency to make their puppets as close as possible to human reality" (1967: 7). Malík's condemnation of today's performers is not that they are guilty of re-creating the live theatre, but, rather, that they are guilty of attempting to imitate human reality itself.

Let us pause to contemplate puppet theatre as a re-creation of live theatre. There is no doubt that such re-creation was extremely common, at least in the West. Jurkowski informs us that "references in Poland indicate that Italians in 1666 performed one day as comedians and another day as puppeteers," presenting precisely the same show (1988 [1983]: 71). But even if the show was the same, is it possible that the audience was unaware of what it was seeing? Even if the puppet-artists attempted to imitate the design, movement, and speech of the live actors in every way possible, still, their imitation could only be imperfect, and the puppets could not be mistaken for the live actors. Whatever else the show offered its audience, there was now the added pleasure, or displeasure, of seeing puppets attempt to perform as if they were live actors. This is not to suggest that such re-creation is a good thing; but surely it is not a simple thing, to be dismissed as merely derivative. The re-creation of live theatre is complicated by the fact that puppets, after all, are not people.

Let us also contemplate the matter of the puppet's re-creation of live theatre from a global perspective. Among the examples given in the introduction, only that of the British "Punch and Judy" performance might be identified as a latter-day, miniature re-creation of a live theatre tradition, that of the commedia dell'arte. And in fact, as Speaight emphasizes, the Punch tradition took on its classic form only when it combined its commedia dell'arte roots with indigenous English roots, which might well have been of greater significance to its structure and characterizations (1990 [1955]: 218–30). It may well be argued that the traditions of puppet theatre represented in the examples from Nigeria, Java, Japan, and India either preceded or were contemporaneous with local live theatre traditions. As Malkin notes in this last case: "A complete history of India's theater would be largely a history of India's complex and diverse forms of puppet theater" (1975: 4). Similar points might be made concerning many non-Western puppet traditions. The commonplace observation that the puppet is an imitation of live theatre is true, perhaps, of much European puppetry in previous ages. It is not true, however, of the general phenomenon of the puppet; puppetry seems often to have been original in itself, rather than derivative of live theatre.

But, as Malík suggests, the miniature re-creation of live theatre is not an immediate problem, in that it is not often practiced these days, when movies and television regularly bring theatrical performance to the most remote hinterlands of the world. One finds almost universal agreement with the proposition offered by the pioneering Russian puppet-artist Nina Efimova: "The puppet theatre must not ever, ever be a miniature reproduction of the big theatre, having its own laws made by its own conditions" (1935: 106).

Rather, the problem since the turn of the century has been with the puppet as an imitation of human life. Such imitation can be characterized as the desire of the puppet-artist to have the puppet be as lifelike in design, movement, and speech as possible. Vsevelod Meyerhold, in an essay that implores actors to "find scope for personal creativity," makes this extended reference to puppetry:

> There are two puppet theatres: the director of the first wants his puppets to look and behave like real men. . . . In his attempts to reproduce reality "as it really is," he improves the puppets further and further until he finally arrives at a far simpler solution to the problem: replace the puppets with real men.
>
> The other director realizes that his audience enjoys . . . [the puppet's] actual movements and poses which, despite all attempts to reproduce life on the stage, fail to resemble exactly what the spectator sees in real life. . . .
>
> I have described these two puppet theatres in order to make the actor consider whether he should assume the servile role of the puppet . . . or whether he should create a theatre like the one in which the puppet stood up for itself and did not yield to the director's efforts to transform it. The puppet did not want to become an exact replica of man, because the world of the puppet is a wonderland of make-believe, and the man which it impersonates is a make-believe man. (1969 [1913]: 128–29)

If the value of imitation from life was once generally accepted by puppet-artists, and if there remains a tendency toward it in the puppet theatre of today, as Malík complains, still, most leading puppet-artists and scholars are united in deprecation of it. As Larry Engler, a noted American performer, writes:

> Puppets that attempt to imitate human movements often create a superficial sense of realism. Once this novelty has worn off, the audience usu-

ally becomes aware of the difference between puppet actions and human actions. Puppets that create the illusion of life by using movements exclusive to their construction can more easily encourage an audience to accept the living existence of an otherwise inanimate object. (1973: 16)

Baird states, with even more emphasis: "When puppeteers try to copy the human animal, they fail. The mechanical copy of life may be amazing, curious, or even frightening, but it doesn't live, whereas the *suggestion* contained in a puppet may be full of life" (1965: 15).

Engler and Baird are surely correct in suggesting that the possibilities for puppetry are limited when the intention is simply to imitate, and that puppetry is far livelier when free to "create the illusion of life" by suggestion. However, it should be recalled that, within such theatrical limitations, the imitative puppet can provide pleasure not only by the verisimilitude of its imitation, but by its very act of imitation, including its failures of verisimilitude. The audience is free to enjoy the attempt at the dramatic scene as well as the dramatic scene itself.

The puppet's ability to represent through imitation is not only limiting to puppetry, it is also only a limited aspect of puppetry. Such imitation might be useful in satire and parody, as in the example from Nigeria, where such elements are central to the performance; but even in satire and parody it is not always found, as we see in "Punch and Judy," where, despite that show's use of parody, there is no attempt at realistic imitation.

And, of course, the desire for verisimilitude is certainly not involved in every puppet performance, as shown in our examples from Japan, India, and Java. The Japanese show disavowed imitation of reality by allowing the audience to see the movers of and the speakers for the puppets, and by having those puppets move and speak in highly formalized ways. The Indian and Javanese shows disavowed such imitation by allowing off-stage puppets to hang lifelessly in full view of the audience. In addition, in the Indian show, the puppets were given distorted and unnatural speech, and in the Javanese show, they exhibited a highly stylized form of movement.

It will be recalled that the subject matter of fantasy is, along with satire and parody, one at which the puppet is particularly adept; and while satire and parody are predicated on imitation, albeit in a distorted and exaggerated form, fantasy can scarcely be said to involve any imitation of reality. The Devil appears late in the "Punch and Judy" show, an ogre in the Indian show, and "living" numbers in the American show; can such fantastic characters actually be imitated in any meaningful sense?

Miles Lee, a performer from Great Britain, develops Meyerhold's argument that there are two approaches to the puppet theatre. The first is based on imitation, while "the other approach is impressionistic. Its aim is not to give a photographic picture but an interpretation. This is achieved by the selection, exaggeration, and distortion of significant characteristics. It exists not to win approval by its technical cleverness but to express a poetic idea or emotion" (1958: 35).

This "other" approach of Lee's follows up on Meyerhold's "other" puppet theatre, and is the one that most contemporary puppetry, and much traditional puppetry in non-European cultures, have chosen to follow. The word impressionistic, however, has not received general acceptance as a description of this approach. Indeed, no single word has gained general acceptance. We saw earlier that Obraztsov writes about the puppet as a generalization, while others refer to the puppet as a symbol. Stantscho Gerdjikov, former director of the Sofia (Bulgaria) Puppet Theatre, offers yet another term when he writes that "the puppet has an indisputable advantage over all other actors: its innate and unlimited possibilities for stylization" (1967 [1965]: 42).

It would only be fair to note, in passing, that this is not an "indisputable advantage" as much as it is a difference in the relative strengths of puppets and live actors. It is unclear whether Gerdjikov means to take the argument as far as would Craig, who suggests that "the body of man is *by nature* utterly useless as a material for an art" (1911: 61). If it is easy to point out the limitations of the live actor, it is just as easy to suggest commensurate limitations for the puppet. But without going to extremes, the point is still well taken: the "possibilities for stylization" are certainly inherent in the puppet, for the artist is free to create the puppet as he or she chooses.

The terms impressionism, generalization, symbolism, and stylization are all intended to describe the nonimitative approach to puppetry; but what is actually being described? It will be worthwhile to analyze the means by which both the imitative and this "other" approach operate.

Imitation from life would have the abstracted signs that constitute the puppet be as lifelike in quality and quantity as possible. Thus the design of an imitative human puppet would include the appropriate anatomical details, such as eyes, nose, limbs, and so on, represented and proportioned in a lifelike manner. The movement of this puppet would be as free from evidence of the mechanical as possible, so that the puppet itself seemed responsible for its motivation, and would include as great a level of detail, such as rolling eyes, a moving mouth, hands that could grasp, as possible. Finally, the speech of this puppet would be the normal human speech appropriate to it, delivered in such a manner that the puppet itself seemed responsible for its delivery.

The "other" approach to the puppet — impressionistic, symbolic, and so on — willfully avoids the attempt at imitation; but it has no new or different means of representation available to it. Abstracted signs of life, within the three sign-systems of design, movement, and speech, are still the means by which the puppet purports to have life. In this "other" approach, however, these signs are not given an especially lifelike quality: the eyes might be orange buttons, the hands grossly oversized; the movement might be obviously mechanical, the speech presented from an obviously external source. Also, the abstracted signs of life are not given in a lifelike quantity: the head might consist of nothing more than a sphere with a notional nose, the legs not exist at all; the puppet might be allowed only a limited range of movement and speech, or be denied one of them entirely.

These, then, are the differences between the two approaches: the imitative approach uses abstracted signs of life in such quality and quantity as to simulate life as closely as possible; the "other" approach uses abstracted signs of life of varied quality and limited quantity, realizing that true simulation is impossible.

Following from this analysis, if the one approach is called imitative, the other may be called conceptual, in that the puppet is given abstracted signs of life of a quality that present the concept of more fully realistic signs, and of a quantity that present the concept of the full quotient of realistic signs. All of the various terms for the nonimitative puppet devolve, essentially, to the puppet's conceptual, as opposed to imitative, capacity.

But the polarity between these two approaches, which would seem to exist regardless of what we called the "other" approach, is a false one, and arises only out of the desire of many involved in puppetry to anathematize imitation. In fact, the means available to all puppet-artists are the same: the quality and the quantity of abstracted signs. Imitative and conceptual puppets are but the extreme poles of what may be called the puppet's continuum of representation. The location of any puppet along this continuum depends on the quality and quantity of the abstracted signs with which the artist invests it.

An explanation of the puppet based on its representational nature follows from this analysis. In each of the performance examples given earlier, the puppets most certainly represent, through the quality and quantity of their abstracted signs, characters that range the continuum from the imitative to the conceptual. As representations, the puppets are invested with any quality or quantity of abstracted signs, and this investiture encourages the audience to imagine the puppets as having life.

An explanation of the puppet as representation also has the virtue of suggesting a basic way in which puppetry is distinct from live theatre. As Gerdjikov and others suggest, the puppet-artist can consciously invest the puppet with abstracted signs of life of the quality and quantity he or she chooses; the live actor might take on mannerisms and disregard aspects of the signifying possibilities of acting, but nonetheless he or she is limited in the choices that might be made, being unable to escape human physiognomy. The actor's appearance can be designed only so much before exhausting the arts of makeup and costume; the actor's motion can occur only in the manner that bones and muscles will allow, even with the aid of mechanical contrivance; and the actor's speech can be delivered only with so much variation of voice, and, in general, is delivered only by the actor.

Even more important, the live actor, despite all of his or her possible exertions, remains but an actor: a person pretending to be another person. Obraztsov suggests that the power of the puppet "lies in the very fact that it is inanimate. . . . On stage, a man might portray another man but he cannot portray man in general because he is himself a man. The puppet is not a man and for that very reason it can give a living portrayal of man in general" (1967 [1965]: 19). It is this general representative capacity of the puppet, as much as its capacity to represent through particular abstracted signs, that appealed at one time to Maurice Maeterlinck, who "felt that human actors, because they were restricted by their physical characteristics, were not appropriate vehicles to portray the archetypical figures with which he peopled his stage" (Knapp 1975: 77).

Is the puppet's particular nature as a representational object the single quality that explains its enduring appeal? Perhaps it is best described as necessary to such an explanation, but not sufficient for it.

Wherever the puppet's deployed signs might be located on the continuum of representation, the audience's perception of the puppet as an object remains unchanging. The puppet's powers of representation allow it to represent characters of the real world and of the imaginary world through the quality and quantity of its abstracted signs of life. But to focus on the puppet as an "object" constituted of those signs, whether in the particular or the general, does not give full credit to the puppet as a "living" dramatic character. To suggest that the enduring appeal of the puppet can be explained by its ability to represent life begs the question of why the audience is willing to translate the representations of the object into that life.

Although we have identified a particular manner of representation as a constant in all puppet performance, this constant, by itself, cannot be the single quality that explains the appeal of the puppet. Puppetry involves something more than just the representative capacity of the puppet. And that something concerns the audience's imagination of life for the puppet.

EXPLANATIONS BASED UPON THE AUDIENCE

The audience of a puppet performance does something that seems, upon examination, to be extraordinary: for the duration of the performance, it chooses to imagine, at least to a certain degree, that the objects presented before it on-stage have life. As we have seen, the puppet encourages this act of imagination by making use of abstracted signs of life. But the imagination of life does not necessarily follow from its representation. Perhaps the single quality that can explain the enduring appeal of the puppet concerns the audience's willingness to make the leap from the perception of representative abstractions to the imagination of life.

McPharlin notes two traditional solutions to this problem before supplying one of his own:

> The puppet has exercised a fascination for mankind since the invention of theatre. . . . It may have something of maternal feeling if puppets are dolls which have deserted the nursery to go on the stage, as Charles Nodier believed [*Revue de Paris,* November, 1842]; it may have something of religious awe if they be the progeny of divine images . . . as Charles Magnin preferred to think [Magnin 1862]. . . . But when they become alive in their theatre the overwhelming appeal is that of theatre only. (1938: 1)

It will be best to begin with McPharlin's solution, that the puppet's "overwhelming appeal is that of theatre only." In a later work he elaborates on this view: "When puppets come alive . . . one ceases to think of wood and wire; one is absorbed in the action. . . . The audience, accepting the convention of puppets, projects itself into them with the same empathy that it feels for any other actors" (1949: 1). Thus, the "life" of the puppet is not, in fact, problematic at all, but is merely the acceptance of a particular theatrical convention.

One is reminded of Coleridge's famous statement about his poetry:

> My endeavours [are] directed to persons and characters supernatural, or at least romantic; yet so as to transfer from our inward nature a human interest and a semblance of truth sufficient to procure for these shadows of imagination that willing suspension of disbelief for the moment, which constitutes poetic faith. (1951 [1817]: 527)

McPharlin seems to have this "willing suspension of disbelief" in mind when he suggests that the audience, "accepting the convention of pup-

pets," thinks not of the actual nature of the puppet, but "projects itself
into them with the same empathy that it feels for any other actors."

Coleridge coined the phrase "suspension of disbelief" to describe his
own poetry, as opposed to that of William Wordsworth; he later applied it to the workings of the theatre. In his survey, *Theories of the
Theatre*, Marvin Carlson notes that Coleridge, in "Progress of the
Drama,"

> speaks of a "combination of several, or of all the fine arts to a harmoni-
> ous whole having a distinct end of its own," this end being that "of imi-
> tating reality (objects, actions, or passions) under the semblance of
> reality." The key word is "semblance," and this requires a contribution
> from the spectator. Plays "are to produce a sort of temporary half-faith,
> which the spectator encourages in himself and supports by a voluntary
> contribution on his own part." (1984: 221)

For McPharlin, "the willing suspension of disbelief," or, alternately, "a
temporary half-faith," works in two steps: the audience accepts the
puppet as if it were a live actor, just as the live actor is accepted as if he
or she were the character being represented; thus, the puppet-as-live-
actor is accepted as the represented character.

McPharlin wants to legitimize the puppet as an instrument of theatre, and feels, perhaps, that such legitimacy can be maintained only if
the distinction between the puppet and the live actor is abolished. Certainly the audience can feel as much empathy for the puppet as for the
live actor; but does the audience ever completely "cease to think of
wood and wire"? Coleridge suggests that in live theatre, the audience
accepts the actor, without difficulty, as the represented character;
McPharlin suggests likewise that, in puppetry, the audience accepts the
puppet, without difficulty, as the represented character. Coleridge's
suggestion is problematic enough; McPharlin's requires the audience to
deny what is plainly before its eyes. In live theatre, a person represents a
person, while in puppetry, an object represents a person: the manner of
representation is fundamentally different.

The power of theatrical convention is not without limit, and if it
seems extreme to suggest that any audience would deny what is plainly

before its eyes, it seems absurd to suggest that every audience is willing to make such a denial. As has been suggested, the replacement of the actor with the puppet is anything but neutral: no audience member above the age of five will be able to overlook completely the essential fact that the puppet has no real life. For this reason, McPharlin's solution, that the audience accepts the puppet conventionally, and responds to it as it would respond to a live actor, cannot be maintained.

One might come at this issue from another direction. If, as McPharlin argues, there is no fundamental difference between the audience's acknowledgment of the actor and of the puppet, then what is gained by the use of the puppet instead of the actor? This question becomes especially acute when puppets are employed in dramas written for actors, such as Shakespearean drama. Why should the artist choose to employ puppets, and the audience desire to see puppets, if the drama is known to work perfectly well with actors? Only some fundamental difference between the puppet and the actor can account for the impulse to employ and to see the one as opposed to the other. The powers of theatrical convention are certainly involved in puppetry, but not in the same manner as they are involved in the live theatre.

There is an interesting variation on the argument of convention, which is implicit not only in McPharlin, but in some of the previously discussed solutions as well. This variation holds that in the conventional, artificial world of the theatre, only a conventional, artificial actor is appropriate.

When a live actor is surrounded by what are obviously nothing more than props and flats, he or she can seem ludicrous, taking seriously what no audience would so take; here indeed some willing suspension of disbelief is required, and here indeed is a common problem in live theatrical representation. Solutions tend in either of two directions: to render the staging materials as realistically as possible, or to dispense with them altogether, relying instead on suggestive description and mime. But there remain practical limitations to stage realism on the one hand, while, on the other hand, the utter absence of props and scenery can leave the actor looking naked on the stage.

Another solution, dating back to Greek tragedy, is to render the actor as unrealistically as possible, through the use of such devices as masks and costumes. In fact, this rendering goes beyond the mere appearance of the actor: as the classical scholar John Jones suggests, "the root function of the so-called megaphone in the Greek dramatic mask is surely to change the voice, not to amplify it" (1980 [1962]: 44). The problem remains, however, that the live actor is of a different nature than his or her theatrical environment: the actor is a living person, albeit one pretending to be some other person, while the theatrical environment remains resolutely theatrical.

László Halász, a psychologist associated with the Budapest State Puppet Theatre, suggests that "the contradiction which is always present between the 'naturalistic' living actor and the anti-naturalistic sets designed by artists ceases to exist in the puppet world; here the anti-naturalistic puppet character and the anti-naturalistic surroundings merge in perfect harmony" (1978: 59). The puppet's remove from reality is in harmony with the remove from reality of its theatrical environment. This might be the quality that explains the puppet's persistence: the puppet intrinsically conforms to the artificiality of the theatre, wherein, by convention, the audience is willing to imagine the puppet as having life, just as it is willing to imagine the theatrical environment to represent the play's reality.

Among the examples given earlier, the most sophisticated of the productions lend credence to this solution: in both the Japanese and American performances, unique theatrical worlds were established, integrating puppets and environment in a manner that could not be duplicated by the live theatre. The less sophisticated of our examples, however, exposed a serious limitation of this argument: in neither the English nor the Nigerian performances was any substantial theatrical environment created, for in each case the use of props and/or scenery was severely limited. If little environment is created, how can the puppet's integration with the theatrical environment be of central importance?

Deszö Szilágyi, director and "theoretician" of the Budapest Puppet Theatre, contends that integration is not, in fact, a sufficient explanation:

> For a long time it was argued that puppetry was the ideal integrated art.
> . . . True enough, this . . . provides a particular enjoyment for the spec-

tator. But the basic prerequisite for this refined aesthetic appreciation is the existence of an appropriate culture. If this is so, why then does the puppet have such an elemental and powerful impact on an unsophisticated audience, mainly on children? The answer must be that in puppetry it is not the aesthetic experience that is the primary factor, but the puppet's immediate psychological impact. (1967 [1965]: 35)

Szilágyi uses the term "aesthetic experience" as if this were something that can come only of vast sophistication; the term may be used in a simpler, more fundamental sense. His contention, however, is well taken: puppetry can make great use of, but does not require, integration of the conventions of the puppet and the theatre. Rather, the puppet has a broader psychological impact upon every type of audience, sophisticated or not. That impact might be recognized in the two theories that McPharlin mentions, only to disregard without further comment: the puppet as "progeny of divine image," and the puppet as a doll that has "deserted the nursery."

The argument that the puppet owes its enduring appeal to its derivation from the religious figure receives its most enthusiastic support from Craig: "To-day, in [the puppet's] least happy period many people regard him as rather a superior doll—and to think he has developed from the doll. This is incorrect. He is a descendent of the stone images of the old temples—he is to-day a rather degenerate form of a god" (1911: 82).

This argument of the puppet's descent is debatable. No doubt that many cultures have used inanimate figures in worship and ritual; it may be doubted, however, whether the moving or speaking religious figure is in fact the progenitor of the puppet, or is simply a figure given movement or speech in a manner similar to that of the puppet. Nonetheless, the obvious similarity between the two suggests that the religious figure might indeed lend to the puppet something of its sacred aura.

Certain types of puppets seem especially reminiscent of the religious figure: the sheer formal stature of greater-than-life-size and near-life-size puppets can suggest the presence of deity; the slow and stately movement of the marionette can suggest the dignity of the divine; and the flickering appearance of the shadow-puppet can suggest the shadow of a god upon the face of the world. The very smallness of the hand-puppet, however, with its penchant for fast and furious activity, makes it hard to imagine the hand-puppet as partaking of any such elevation, unless we are to take it as some imp or devil.

Or perhaps it is not any physical resemblance between the puppet and the religious figure that entwines the two, but rather a metaphorical association: as the gods endow life in, and exercise control over the lives of humanity, so humanity endows and controls the puppet's "life." This takes us rather far afield from Craig's anthropological speculations, but seems more convincing. Although many audiences for puppetry have little involvement with religious figures, and can scarcely be expected to recall in the puppet any idolatrous or ritualistic origins, all such audiences have some notion, however attenuated, of the life-giving and controlling power of the gods, and could associate the puppet with this.

The problem with this associative argument is that it is not sufficiently ample to accommodate the diversity of puppetry. Its limitations are exposed by our Nigerian and English examples. The former, with its emphasis on satire, and the latter, with its outrageous mischief, seem oblivious to any religious interpretation, despite Punch's battle with the Devil. Are audiences led to reflect upon the divine by lewdly satirical representations of copulation and grossly comical representations of murder?

If the supposed religious descent of the puppet is a noble one, the supposed ascent of the puppet from the nursery doll is unhappily ignoble. Such an ascent would suggest, to Craig as well as others, that the puppet is little more than an overdeveloped child's toy. In light of this, most puppet-artists accord the argument little credence, and follow McPharlin and Craig in offering but a few words of disparagement before moving on.

As with the religious argument, the argument that the puppet has enduring appeal owing to its derivation from the nursery doll does not, ultimately, depend on any proof that the puppet is literally ascended from the doll. Such an ascent is as likely or unlikely as a descent from the religious figure. Rather, the argument is based on the obvious similarity of certain types of puppets to the child's doll, and suggests that the doll might lend to the puppet something of its personal charm.

Earlier, in analyzing definitions of the puppet, a distinction was made between the puppet and the doll on the basis of the theatrical usage of the puppet; such a distinction does not deny the similarity between the two, but points up their differing functions, with the doll having only a private one. It remains to be seen whether the puppet's charms are derived from those of the doll.

Certain types of puppets seem especially reminiscent of the doll: the small size and simple movements of the hand-puppet can evoke in the audience a remembrance of childhood toys; rod-puppets and hand-and-rod puppets, although larger, are still scaled down from life in a doll-like manner. But other types of puppets seem to defy such reminiscence. Smallness, of course, is not an invariable characteristic of the puppet; near-life-size and larger-than-life-size puppets can scarcely be considered doll-like, and tend to be anything but charming. Also, the physical distance between the puppet-operator and the marionette, as well as certain other types of puppets, seems very unlike the proximal relationship between the child and the doll.

Or perhaps it is not any physical resemblance between the puppet and the doll that binds them in the imagination, but rather a metaphorical association similar to that advanced in the religious argument: as the child believes in, and exercises control over, the charmed life of the doll, so humanity believes in and controls the charming puppet's "life." Despite the low regard with which this argument is held, it seems to have as much validity as the religious argument. Although many audiences for puppetry are far removed from playing with dolls, all such audiences have some notion, however attenuated, of the life-giving and controlling power of childhood fantasy, and might associate the puppet with this.

The problem with this associative argument is that it also is insufficiently ample to accommodate the puppet's diversity. Its limitations are exposed in our Japanese and American performance examples. The former, with its insistently formal representations of life, is worlds away from the charming power of childhood belief, while the latter, despite its representations of life growing directly out of the child's imagination, scorns the very idea that the child has any control over them. Are audiences led to remember the charm of childhood dolls

while viewing an intense portrayal of a double suicide or of a child being mocked by the figures of his imagination?

The arguments that the puppet descends from the religious figure or
ascends from the nursery doll are, on first impression, mutually contra-
dictory; but as we have seen, the actual lineage of the puppet, one way
or the other, is not as important as the metaphorical associations that
the puppet invites in its audience. The associations suggested by these
arguments are similar, in that both are concerned with man's willful
imagination and control of the puppet's "life" through association with
either the religious figure or the nursery doll. Although neither of these
arguments suggests a single quality that explains the appeal of the puppet, the underlying metaphorical association that they share is pregnant
with meaning. In the coda to this study, we will examine in more detail this matter of metaphor and the puppet; for now, it will be sufficient to note that the puppet as a metaphor for humanity has been cited
in cultures widely separated in time and space.

Otakar Zich, a Czech semiotician, offers an analysis of the audience's
response to the puppet that contains curious echoes of these arguments
about the puppet's appeal, but his point is of a different nature entirely:

> The puppets may be perceived either as living people or as lifeless dolls.
> Since we can perceive them *only* one way at a time, we are faced with
> two possibilities:
>
> a) We perceive the puppets as dolls [and] stress their inanimate charac-
> ter. It is the material they are made of that strikes us as something that
> we are really perceiving. In that case . . . we cannot take seriously their
> speech or their movements . . . hence, we find them comical and gro-
> tesque. . . . We perceive them as figurines, but they demand we take
> them as people; and this invariably amuses us. . . .
>
> b) [Or] . . . we may conceive of the puppets as if they were living
> beings by emphasizing their lifelike expressions, their movements and
> speech, and taking them as real. Our awareness that the puppets are
> not alive recedes, and we get the feeling of something inexplicable,
> enigmatic, and astounding. In this case, the puppets seem to act myste-
> riously. . . . Here we are faced with something utterly unnatural—
> namely, life in an inanimate, inorganic material. (quoted in Bogatyrev
> 1983 [1973]: 48)

Zich's first possibility of perception seems related to the argument that the audience associates the puppet with the nursery doll, while his second possibility seems related to the argument that the audience associates the puppet with the religious figure. In fact, his point is more subtle yet more dogmatic: whatever associations the audience might make, the puppet can be taken only as either "comic and grotesque" or "inexplicable [and] enigmatic."

Bogatyrev makes a number of criticisms of Zich's analysis (1983 [1973]: 49–62), and they themselves are criticized by Jurkowski (1988 [1983]: 57–61) and Veltruský (1983: 108–9). Veltruský writes, however, that one criticism "remains valid, namely, that there exist puppet performances that are neither comic nor mysterious, but simply serious" (1983: 109). This criticism, even if it must stand alone, is devastating: Zich suggests that an audience can view the puppet in only two ways, and he is plainly wrong. Our example from Japan suggests that its audience perceives the puppets as neither "comic and grotesque" nor "inexplicable [and] enigmatic," but, in Veltruský's words, as "simply serious." Zich's either/or theory fails to account for the puppet in all its diversity; the appeal of the puppet need not be either one way or the other. There remains Zich's point that the puppet can be seen in "*only one way at a time.*" Is this, indeed, the case? We will be returning to this crucial point in the next chapter.

For the moment, we remain concerned with the appeal of the puppet, and it will be best to consider the most fundamental level of audience involvement. Miles Lee, a British performer and author, writes that "a puppet, however cunningly manipulated by the puppeteer, is never fully alive until given additional stimulus through the imagination of its audience" (1958: 8). Only the imaginative contribution of the audience allows the puppet to have "life." This is surely the point where the "temporary half-faith" suggested by Coleridge applies to puppetry, but it is a half-faith different than that applied to the live theatre.

Heinrich von Kleist, in his famous and enigmatic essay, "On the Marionette Theatre," suggests that, as opposed to the live actor, the puppet possesses a special grace that arises from its lack of consciousness (1978 [1810]: 1212). This implies the further suggestion that such consciousness needs to be supplied by the audience. Maeterlinck, perhaps intentionally, makes this implication explicit in his belief that puppets "come to life only when the spectator projects his unconscious content onto them" (Knapp 1975: 77). One could quibble with the semantics of "unconscious content," but the suggestion seems correct. The puppet is but an object constituted of abstracted signs in the perception of the audience; the audience must give meaning to these signs by an act of imagination, according a sense of life to the puppet in response to its abstracted signs. Otherwise, the puppet will remain only an object, regardless of the quality and quantity of those signs.

But if this is the case, it remains to be seen why the audience is prepared to lend its imaginative will to the puppet: why should an audience bother to project its consciousness, to imagine life? As we have seen, the metaphorical associations of the puppet with the religious figure and the childhood doll offer two possible reasons, although neither is sufficient on its own; together, however, they lead to a suggestion that the power of metaphor has a general psychological impact on the audience, making the audience desirous of according the puppet its "life."

Szilágyi contends that there are two aspects to the puppet's psychological impact: "(1) On the puppet stage, before the spectator's eyes, the supreme act of creation is taking place—lifeless, dead matter is turned into life. . . . (2) The puppet . . . no matter in what form it may appear, is, deep down in the human mind, a primordial symbol of the human being" (1967 [1965]: 35). The metaphorical associations involving the puppet as religious figure and as childhood doll are here united and enfolded into a more general psychological association. The audience is willing to imagine the puppet as having life because to do so fulfills the basic human desire to understand the world through the prism of human consciousness. The puppet's lack of consciousness as a perceived object is thus an invitation for the audience to participate in the creation of "life" similar to its own.

Is the psychological desire to imagine life the synchronic explanation of the puppet for which we have been seeking? Perhaps it can best be described, as was the explanation of puppet as representative "object," as necessary, but not sufficient, for such an explanation.

The psychological desire that leads the audience to imagine that the puppet has life is not, in fact, operative only with the puppet: as we have seen, religious figures, in themselves, and childhood dolls, in themselves, can just as easily be imagined as having life. Indeed, life may be imagined as inhering in the house that sits across the street, in the smoke that curls up from a cigarette or pipe, or even in the computers upon which people write. The half-shuttered windows of the house may be the sleepy eyes of a hulking giant; the wraithlike smoke of the pipe may be the vaporous form of some spirit of the air; the performance of complex tasks by the computer may be the product of intelligence; yet none of these things, as they exist, are in any way puppets. Religious figures, dolls, houses, pipe smoke, computers, along with a myriad other commonplaces of the world, are all without consciousness, yet all present, most often without the least intention, signs that may be imagined to indicate life. If the psychological desire to imagine life explains the puppet's enduring appeal, it follows not only that everything can be a puppet, but that everything is a puppet, which is absurd.

The psychological desire to imagine life can be characterized as promiscuous — willing to lavish its attention on every object that happens into view, rather than to limit its attention to the more specific "object" of the puppet. More than that, this promiscuity of desire obliterates the actual perception of the object in favor of its imagined life; the object itself is rendered mere stimulus for imaginative joy.

It will be recalled that McPharlin argues that the audience responds through convention to the puppet as if it were a live actor, that is, as a dramatic character, and that this argument fails because it ignores the actual "object" of the puppet. The argument of psychological desire, although more subtle and persuasive, ultimately falls prey to the same weakness: the focus remains on the "life" of the puppet as a dramatic character, and overlooks the particular way in which that imagination of life is stimulated. To suggest that the enduring appeal of the puppet can be explained by its ability to foster the imagination of life begs the question of how the puppet is in any significant manner an object that differs from many other objects in the world.

Thus, although we have isolated the constant in all puppet performance of the audience's psychological desire for the puppet to have life, this constant, by itself, is not the single quality that explains the puppet. Just as puppetry involves something more than the puppet's representative capacity as perceived object, it also involves something more than the audience's desire to imagine that the puppet has life. That something more can be identified when we consider the perception along with the imagination, the "object" along with the "life."

3

A NEW BASIS FOR DEFINITION AND EXPLANATION

The reader will, no doubt, have noticed a symmetry between the necessary but insufficient solutions proposed at the conclusions of the last two sections of the preceding chapter. The first solution is that the puppet's enduring and widespread appeal derives from its distinctive ability as an "object" to deploy representative abstracted signs, while the second is that the puppet's appeal derives from its distinctive ability to satisfy the audience's desire to imagine life as pervading the world. A synchronic explanation of the appeal of the puppet, an explanation that will apply to every manifestation of theatrical puppetry, will need to be aware of both of these aspects; it will need to account for the puppet's dual nature as representative perceived object and as psychologically imagined life.

DOUBLE-VISION

It will be useful to return to Otakar Zich, who argues, as we have seen, that the audience can perceive the puppet in either of two ways, as inanimate doll or as living being. To avoid confusion with the specialized use of the word perception throughout this study, let us restate for Zich that the audience can acknowledge the puppet as either inanimate doll or living being. Are not these two ways essentially the two aspects of the puppet's nature as "object" and as "life"? Zich argues that the acknowledgment of the puppet by the audience is an either/or proposition. But can the audience, in fact, acknowledge "the puppet *only* one way at a time," as Zich insists? Zich's argument was criticized earlier for its failure to account for puppetry that was neither "comical and grotesque," as when the puppet is acknowledged as an inanimate doll, nor "enigmatic and astounding," as when the puppet is acknowledged as a living being. The criticism now is that these two types of acknowledgment are not necessarily antithetical. Is it not possible for the audience to acknowledge the puppet in both ways at once?

Thomas Green and W. J. Pepicello, American scholars of theatre and linguistics, suggest that the audience's acknowledgment is not exclusively a matter of either/or:

> While the audience knows, on some level, that the puppet is a mere sign (specifically a metonym), observers are led to disattend this fact by the artistic conventions of the art form. . . . [Yet] despite the convention of disattending the human presence in puppet plays, some traditions . . . [create a] tension arising from the audience's alternate perception of the puppet as an independent "actor" and as a manipulated object. (1983: 155)

Green and Pepicello argue that the audience "disattends" two distinct things: the puppet "as a mere sign," and "the human presence in puppet plays," presumably the more or less obvious fact that puppets are moved and accorded speech by humans. The former, it seems, is always disattended, while the latter is not disattended in "some traditions," such as Japanese Bunraku, that make no attempt to hide the fact of human involvement. In these traditions, Green and Pepicello note an oscillation in the audience's acknowledgement "between object as actor (i.e., having life) and acted upon (i.e., inanimate object)" (1983: 157). This oscillation is essentially a rapid and recurring shift between Zich's two ways of acknowledging the puppet.

Although this theory offers a significant advance over Zich in allowing for a relationship between the two aspects of the puppet, there are two problems with it. The first is that oscillation between the puppet

as "actor" and "acted upon" is not considered to be universally operative: it is implied that if the puppet-operator is not visible, no such oscillation will occur; the universal disattendance of the puppet as "mere
sign" will predominate, supplemented by the local disattendance of the
invisible puppet-operator. Green and Pepicello imply that the "life" of
the puppet, as expressed through "artistic convention," will be valued
more highly than the nature of the puppet as an "object" constituted of
signs. Or, to put it more simply: without the visible presence of the
puppet-operator, the two aspects of the puppet will not be held in tension.

The second problem is with the conflicting logic of oscillation and
disattendance: oscillation contradicts the suggestion that, while the audience is aware that "on some level" the puppet is "mere sign," this
awareness is ultimately disattended. Either the audience oscillates between the two aspects of the puppet in balanced tension, or the two
aspects are not balanced, and the puppet as "life" dominates the puppet
as "object." Although Green and Pepicello do not attempt to resolve
this contradiction, their limitation of oscillation to puppetry in which
there is the "human presence" of a visible puppet-operator implies that,
as a rule, awareness and disattendance of the puppet as "mere sign" is
the more fundamental acknowledgment of the puppet by the audience.
Again, to put it more simply: oscillation and disattendance are incompatible, and given the choice between them, Green and Pepicello seem
to suggest that disattendance is the more common.

Despite these problems, there is much to be credited to the suggestions of Green and Pepicello. If only in traditions that expose the human presence of the puppet-operator, and if only in a manner that does
not quite allow for simultaneous acknowledgment of the puppet's dual
nature, they help to break down Zich's imposing either/or.

Jurkowski goes further. He does not limit the acknowledgment of
the puppet's dual nature as "object" and "life" to traditions that include
a human presence on-stage. Within "the sign system of the puppet theatre," he notes what he calls "the opalescence of the puppet," meaning
"the double existence of the puppet, which is perceived (and demonstrated) both as puppet and scenic character" (1988 [1983]: 78). Or, as
he explains in another article:

When movement fully dominates an object we feel that the character is
born and present on the stage. When it is the nature of the object which
dominates we still see the object. The object is still the object and the
character at the same time. . . . This is what I mean by "opalisation."
(1988 [1984]: 41)

Thus opalescence, or opalisation, refers to the audience's simultaneous
acknowledgment of the puppet's dual nature, a unity of acknowledgment; or, in the terms of this study, a tension between the puppet's two
aspects of "object" and "life." Although this is yet a further advance
over Zich, there is a problem here as well.

Quite simply, Jurkowski does not consider opalisation to be inherent
in the puppet itself. He argues that it has been operative only since the
inception of what he calls the "sign system of the puppet theatre":
"The puppet has been producing this opalisation effect since the
eighteenth century. The puppet was [only] then considered a puppet
and a live character at the same time" (1988 [1984]: 41). We soon will
consider Jurkowski's discussion of the various "sign systems" in which
the puppet might be employed; for the moment, it is enough to note
that in the contexts of "neighboring sign systems" and the "sign system of the live theatre," Jurkowski believes the puppet to be acknowledged only as, respectively, "object" or "life." Opalescence, then, is not
inherent in all puppet performance, but only in a certain style of such
performance. According to Jurkowski, Zich's either/or was abolished
only in the period when that style of performance became current in
the West.

Péter Molnár Gál, a designer for the Budapest State Puppet Theatre,
offers no explanatory term of his own, but succeeds in doing away entirely with Zich's either/or when describing one of his theatre's "distinguishing characteristics":

Everything is what it is, plus something else: a recognizable object and a
transfigured object at the same time. On the puppet stage a feather-
duster may symbolize a fairy prince illumined by glory, but we must
never forget that it still remains a feather-duster. While the objects lose
their original purpose and become transformed into something else,
they still faintly preserve their original character. (1978: 14)

One might quibble over the phrase "faintly preserve," for according to the logic of the description, the aspect of the puppet as "recognizable object" is held in tension with the aspect of the puppet as "transfigured object." Excepting that, Gál is obviously dealing with what Green and Pepicello have called oscillation, and Jurkowski has called opalescence.

Once more, however, simultaneous acknowledgement of the two aspects of the puppet is circumscribed: Gál limits it, if only by implication, to the workings of his own theatre. As he is not attempting to explain puppetry at large, such a limitation is understandable. The Budapest State Puppet Theatre consciously bases its work on the tension inherent in the dual nature of the puppet, and Gál considers this to be his theatre's greatest strength. He does not discuss whether this tension can be found throughout puppet performance.

Finally, let us consider a comment by the brilliant Polish scholar Jan Kott, concerning what he believes to be the most distinctive aspect of Bunraku:

> Bunraku is almost the only puppet theatre in which the mechanism is completely bared. The aesthetics of this art consists in evoking absolute illusion, and in its equally absolute destruction. Bunraku is *simultaneously* a theatre in which puppets act human dramas — cry and laugh, love and hate, cheat, sacrifice themselves, and kill — and a metatheatre, whose protagonists are the manipulators operating the puppets, the narrator, and the [musician]; metatheatre, whose dramatic action consists in revealing the theatrical illusion. (1976: 100)

Again, we seem to be dealing with the same essential idea of oscillation and of opalisation, but now in terms of the puppet's performance being "simultaneously . . . theatre and metatheatre." Clearly, the life that the audience imagines in the puppet is theatre, while the puppet's intentional exposure as a perceived object is metatheatre.

The burden of the foregoing review has been to show that Zich's either/or view is insupportable, and that, in fact, simultaneous acknowledgment of the puppet's two aspects is a defining characteristic of at least certain styles of puppet theatre, or of a certain period of puppet theatre, or of two particular, yet widely divergent, puppet theatres. It remains to be suggested that every puppet, in every age, in every theatre and tradition, invites its audience to acknowledge, at once, its two aspects; and it remains to be suggested that through the tension inherent in this dual acknowledgment, the puppet pleasurably challenges its audience's understanding of what it means to be an "object" and what it means to have "life."

The puppet, properly speaking, exists only as a particular process of performance, in which the audience perceives a theatrical figure to be an object that is made to deploy abstracted signs of life, which encourage the audience to satisfy its psychological desire to imagine that the perceived object does, in fact, have life.

This process is what Green and Pepicello refer to when they write of oscillation, what Jurkowski refers to when he writes of opalisation, what Gál refers to when he writes of the puppet as "a recognizable object and a transfigured object at the same time," and what Kott refers to when he writes of "simultaneous . . . theatre and metatheatre"; contrary to all of these writers, however, this process is not limited within puppetry, but is central to the phenomenon throughout its temporal and geographic diversity.

A precise and self-explanatory term is required as a name for this process. Green and Pepicello's oscillation unnecessarily suggests a continual wavering in the audience's acknowledgment of the two aspects of the puppet. Jurkowski's opalisation, while nicely poetic, requires substantial exegesis to be comprehensible. Gál and Kott fail to provide any term at all. We would call the process double-vision, for, in the course of the performance, the audience sees the puppet, through perception and through imagination, as an object and as a life; that is, it sees the puppet in two ways at once.

A constant tension exists within this double-vision created by the puppet: each of the puppet's aspects is inescapable, and yet each contradicts the other. The puppet is and is not that which it seems to be. Chikamatsu Monzaemon, Japan's most renowned Bunraku playwright, writes that "art is something which lies in the slender margin between the real and the unreal. . . . It is unreal, and yet it is not unreal; it is real, and yet it is not real" (quoted in Brecht 1988 2:706). The art of puppetry certainly lies in this "slender margin," for the audience's acknowledgment of the puppet, through perception and imagination, sets up a conflict between the puppet as object and as life. What may be called the ontological status of the puppet is always within the margin of doubt; its place in that margin is its most distinctive characteristic.

Basil Milovsoroff, a twentieth-century American puppet-artist, muses that "perhaps the puppet's real beauty is its native theatricality" (1976: 5). What is willful in the live theatre is native to the puppet: a process of representation that is inherently make-believe, and is predicated on a double-vision that acknowledges the "object" of the puppet as having "life."

It would be incorrect to say that all puppetry consciously strives to create double-vision; in fact, such a striving has not been central to the phenomenon of the puppet. As we have seen in Jurkowski's example of the Italian theatre company that alternately performed live and with puppets, double-vision might well have frequently been considered an undesirable side effect. Nonetheless, double-vision is a constant in all puppet performance, whether intentionally or not, and thus provides the basis for a synchronic explanation of the puppet's widespread and enduring appeal, for it creates in every audience the pleasure of a profound and illuminating paradox provoked by an "object" with "life."

Thus the suggestions for a definition advanced earlier can now be supplemented with a synchronic explanation of the puppet: the puppet is a theatrical figure, perceived by an audience to be an object, that is given design, movement, and frequently, speech, so that it fulfills the audience's desire to imagine it as having life; by creating a double-vision of perception and imagination, the puppet pleasurably challenges the audience's understanding of the relationship between objects and life.

The paradoxical pleasure created by the puppet's process of double-vision operates on a fundamental level, beneath the more obvious pleasures that are provided by the "object" of the puppet with its abstracted signs of design, movement, and speech, and by the puppet's "life" as a dramatic character within a narrative. Our intention has not been to demean these pleasures, for, in the almost infinite variety of their manifestations, they have conquered countless millions of hearts; rather, our intention has been to demonstrate that beneath them can be found a more complex pleasure, operative throughout puppet performance.

It should not, however, be thought that this more complex pleasure, this pleasure of the ontological paradox, demands of its audience any remarkable level of aesthetic or philosophical reflection. The process of double-vision does not require that the audience be aware of it. And so, while it is true that the puppet makes special demands upon its audience, these demands can easily be met by any audience of kindergarten children. The demands are nothing more than that the audience be receptive to the abstracted signs of life that constitute the puppet, and be desirous of seeing the world through the prism of human consciousness; from such reception and desire, all else will follow.

If anything, a major problem in puppetry is the very ease with which its special demands are met. Peter Arnott, contemplating what he believes to be the low standards all too often found in puppetry, concludes that "there is no doubt that puppetry is fatally easy. There is an irresistible attraction about these little moving figures" (1964: 40). What is "fatally easy" is the inherent ability of the puppet to create the paradoxical pleasure of double-vision: almost regardless of the production values involved, the puppet will stimulate a certain amount of pleasure by challenging its audience to consider the ontology of an "object" with "life."

Arnott suggests that this ease is, ultimately, the reason for which puppetry, at least in the West, has come to be held in low regard:

> When the puppet in itself is so attractive, does it much matter what it does? Thus a vicious cycle is created. The percipient adult comes to realize that he can expect only a superficial entertainment. . . . [He then] expects to be able to bring children, and troupes who make their living from puppetry are forced to give the public what it wants. Inevitably, the entertainment offered cannot rise above a certain level. (1964: 40–41)

The paradoxical pleasure of the puppet's process of double-vision is so easy to create that it can lead to a laziness among puppet-artists. It need only be noted that such laziness, and the mediocre puppetry that results from it, are the fault of particular artists, and not of puppetry itself. As we have seen from our introductory examples, when artists do not fall prey to such laziness they are able to create masterful and important theatrical productions — productions possible only with the puppet.

A TEST OF DOUBLE-VISION

The reader will recall from the introduction that Jurkowski challenges the value of any synchronic approach, arguing that the diachronic diversity of puppetry is such that the puppet can be comprehended only through discussion of its employment in specific theatrical contexts. It will be worthwhile to test the ideas of this study against the various contexts that Jurkowski enumerates. If the puppet as a process of double-vision can be found to be operative in each instance, then double-vision may fairly be claimed to operate synchronically in all theatrical puppetry.

To review briefly: Jurkowski argues that "the presence of a puppet is not always and inevitably constitutive of one fixed sign system of puppet theatre" (1988 [1983]: 67). Rather, the puppet can be put in the service of "neighboring sign systems," the "sign system of the live theatre," the "sign system of the puppet theatre," or a contemporary sign system characterized by "the atomization of all elements of the puppet theatre" (1988 [1983]: 68, 71, 76, 79).

Jurkowski's use of the term sign system is different than the hyphenated term sign-system used in this study: the former refers to comprehensive theatrical systems of signification, as listed above, in which the puppet has been employed; the latter refers to the three specific systems of signification — design, movement, and speech — presented by the puppet. It is unfortunate that the hyphen must bear the weight of distinguishing the two terms, but, for our purposes, the term "sign-system" needs to be distinct from Jurkowski's broader use of the term.

Jurkowski demonstrates the puppet's variety of services in a survey of "the puppet's long journey through different sign systems" in European theatre. He aptly notes that these services, although broadly chronological, not only overlap in time, but coexist today (1988 [1983]: 68).

After a brief review of puppets in classical times, he settles onto the Middle Ages and Renaissance, in which he cites the service of puppets to "neighboring sign systems." After defining theatre to mean "actors (live or puppet) who in a special space present imagined characters, according to a given or improvised drama, being seen by a public gathered especially or by chance," he argues that "puppet demonstrations [of this period] always lacked some elements [of theatre]: they did not have dramas or the puppets were not characters" (1988 [1983]: 68).

Jurkowski cites two particular types of puppet service. First, there were puppets that "tried to be alive like a man. Of course, they could not be alive like a man, and thus they seemed to be caricatures of man." Second, there were puppets "used as illustrations" by "bards and story-tellers," just as "scroll paintings" were used (1988 [1983]: 69).

The first type of service, to a sign system that Jurkowski does not name, but that could be labelled spectacle, is exemplified by "trick puppets," which "included metamorphosis puppets and circus puppets. . . . The metamorphosis puppets were technical accomplishments that were shown as such to surprise the audience. In this they were successful, as were the circus puppets (jugglers, rope dancers, acrobats, and others)" (1988 [1983]: 76). The trick puppet, which survives to this day, makes no pretense of being a character in a drama: it "attempts to be something real, and being real [it becomes] an object of spectacular and public interest" (1988 [1983]: 70). That is, it serves as an object of curiosity. How might double-vision apply to such a usage?

The key lies in Milovsoroff's notion of the puppet's native theatricality. This native quality was discussed earlier; we saw that while the pretense of the actor is to be a particular character, that of the puppet is to be alive. In either case, the pretense involves a make-believe representation. Thus, even if the context of performance is one wherein a live juggler would be engaged in spectacle, as opposed to theatre, the puppet juggler's pretense of life makes it into the character of a living juggler. Although it is only an "object," its abstracted signs, in this case most especially the movements characteristic of juggling, lead the audience to imagine that it has the "life" of a juggler. This pretense creates at least a rudimentary drama, the "performance of a juggler." And so we see that, in fact, we can use the concept of double-vision to identify in the trick puppet both elements of the theatre called for by Jurkowski.

The second type of service cited by Jurkowski is the service provided by the puppet to the neighboring sign system of the story-teller's art. Jurkowski's example comes from Cervantes's *Don Quixote:*

> The Renaissance puppet theater of Master Pedro (Cervantes) is a sort of storyteller performance. A boy stands in front of the *retablo* [puppet stage] and points at the *retablo* puppets while telling the story of don Gaiferos and Melissandra. The boy's text is mostly narration, only occasionally including the words of the acting figures. The principal role of this presentation belongs to the boy; he is the main actor. The *retablo* and its puppets are but illustrations. When necessary the boy responds to remarks made by the audience. He is, then, a real intermediary, but he mediates the reaction of the public towards the text (words) and not towards the puppets. (1988 [1983]: 64)

This usage of the puppet is opposed by Jurkowski to that in performances of "Petrushka" shows, in which a performer acts as an intermediary between the puppet and the audience, playing music and interpreting the puppet's words:

> There is no doubt that in the case of don Pedro's theater, the *retablo* puppet served the actor (storyteller), while in the case of the Petrushka comedy it was the actor (musician) who served the puppets. In the first case the story is the constitutive element of the presentation, in the second one it is the puppet hero. I would dare say that the puppets entered into two quite different sign systems. (1988 (1983): 64–65)

The "two quite different sign systems" are those of the story-teller and of the puppet theatre proper. Jurkowski's point is that this matter of whether the puppet serves or is served changes the audience's comprehension of it, for in Don Pedro's theatre, the puppets only do what a scroll with pictures might do—illustrate the story—and thus lack dramatic character of their own.

And yet the puppets in Don Pedro's theatre are not pictures on a scroll; although their service is similar, it is not the same. The difference is precisely the double-vision created by the puppet. It is crucial to note that when Don Quixote becomes angered by the narrative, he does not attack the story-teller—who, as Jurkowski would have it, is the primary actor in the production—but attacks the puppets. If the story-teller were illustrating his tale with pictures on a scroll, it is difficult to imagine Don Quixote shredding the scroll in his rage; he would attack the story-teller instead. The puppets, although in service to the story-teller, have a significance that far surpasses any that might be had by pictures on a scroll, a significance predicated on the double-vision the puppets provoke.

Don Quixote is, of course, insane; this insanity leads him to value the life he imagines in the puppets over his perception of them as objects. Thus they suffer his attack as the "living" agents of the drama, despite the performance of the story-teller. The presence of the puppet in the place of the scroll is not a neutral event, and again we see that, in fact, both elements of the theatre called for by Jurkowski can be found, using the concept of double-vision, in this usage of the puppet.

Jurkowski follows the puppet into the Baroque and Romantic eras, when it served in the sign system of the live theatre. We have already seen how an Italian company touring in Poland alternately performed live and with puppets. In the Baroque era, puppets performing opera became quite fashionable:

> In announcements of the time, the puppet theatre managers assured the public that their puppets would act like live actors. Today it is hard to believe that a puppet could imitate an actor so perfectly that it might be treated as his miniature. However, this was quite possible in the operatic puppet theatre of the seventeenth century. The acting of live singers and actors at the time was fully schematic. The singers stood in a row at the proscenium opening and made schematic gestures. . . . To imitate such acting was easy for the puppet, especially since the light was not bright and the wire network [hung in front of the stage] hid the [puppet's] strings. (1988 [1983]: 72)

Puppet opera should not be confused with popular theatre, as it was presented for the cultured classes, in cities where live opera was, presumably, available. In addition to puppet-operators, puppet opera productions required a goodly number of singers and musicians. Clearly, purveyors of puppet opera hoped to capitalize on an audience that specifically chose to see "puppets [that] would act like live actors." If the audience understood in advance the nature of the performance, as would generally seem to have been the case, then their attendance was dependent, at least in part, on a desire to see puppets rather than live actors.

The key aspects of Jurkowski's description are the puppet as miniature actor, and the "wire network" that hid the means of puppet operation. The audience was aware that what it saw was not life-sized, and, moreover, that it was not presented without dissimulation. That is to say, the audience was aware that it saw an imitation of live opera, and not the real thing. That such productions were derivative is not in question; nonetheless, it seems clear that the audience acknowledged the puppet as a distinctive theatrical performer, and that they attended puppet opera precisely to take pleasure in that distinction.

Popular puppetry in the sign system of the live theatre came, according to Jurkowski, in two stages:

> The first stage of adaptation covered the Baroque theatre model and the Baroque repertory, including Bible stories, myths, Evangile [sic] parables, hagiographic plays, and two famous Renaissance subjects, "Don Juan" and "Doktor Faust." . . . The second stage of adaptation covered the Romantic repertory and Romantic theatre models. Puppet theatres in Germany, France, Belgium, and Bohemia adapted the repertory, settings, and costumes of melodrama, . . . imitating the live theatre. (1988 [1983]: 75)

Jurkowski does not give an example of puppets in the sign system of the theatre, but an example of his "second stage of adaptation" would seem to be the Liège puppet tradition of Belgium, in which the romance of Charlemagne was presented with splendidly costumed puppets operated from above via stout rods in the puppets' heads.

As with the fashionable puppet opera, popular puppet theatre such as in Liège was in many ways derivative of live theatre; but again, the substitution of puppets for actors inescapably changed the performance. Insofar as popular puppet theatre imitates live theatre, the analysis given of puppet opera demonstrates how the presence of the puppet transforms the imitation into something of a different nature. In fact, however, the Liège tradition went far beyond imitation of the live theatre. Malkin notes that in this tradition "complete play cycles might require eight hundred elaborately carved and costumed figures. Usually it would take several months of performances given in serial fashion to complete the drama" (1977: 24). One might doubt whether the live theatre has ever made use of so many characters over such an extended period of performance. Although the Liège tradition employed certain live theatre conventions, it exploded the conventions of cast size and story length.

And it did more than that. It made use of puppets that were of extremely disparate height. As Malkin explains, "Audiences knew . . . that large figures were stronger or more noble than small figures. In this way, Charlemagne might be nearly five feet tall, while a minor character might be less than eighteen inches high" (1977: 24–25). The use of such variations in height to convey information about characters is, of course, impossible in the theatre of live actors. Thus, we see that even when it serves in what Jurkowski calls the sign system of the live theatre, the puppet invariably differs from the actor, through the careful deployment of its unique resources.

Jurkowski's next stop in the puppet's journey focuses on the hundred years astride the turn of the twentieth century, when puppets, after some pioneering efforts, entered into the sign system of the puppet theatre proper, as "artificial creatures [that] behave in their own typical way" (1988 [1983]: 76–77).

The distinguishing characteristic of this sign system is that it is the puppet that is served, and the particular nature of the puppet that is explored. This nature is what Jurkowski calls opalescence, and it is, as we have seen, similar to our idea of double-vision. As such, it will not be necessary to demonstrate the theatrical distinctiveness of the puppet within this sign system. It will be worthwhile, however, to note two points about the sign system of the puppet theatre, in that it has two distinct manifestations.

First, this sign system is exemplified by certain kinds of traditional puppetry, such as "Punch and Judy" and "Petrushka" shows. The former occasionally, and the latter generally, have a live actor as intermediary between the puppet and the audience. This actor "serves the puppet," assisting in its presentation to the audience.

It is interesting, however, that Jurkowski locates these traditions where he does, in that both share an ancestry traceable at least in part to the live theatre commedia dell'arte, and perhaps even to the live theatre comedy of ancient Rome (Baird 1965: 96, 103). Should they not then be located in the sign system of the live theatre? That they are not is indicative of Jurkowski's schema, in which the most important issue is that of service: in both traditions, it is the puppet that is served. Our introductory example from India, in which a live musician translates for the audience the puppets' semicomprehensible speech, is another example of this service. The boundaries between Jurkowski's sign systems, based only on this matter of service, seem quite tenuous when examined from any other perspective.

Second, the sign system of the puppet theatre is exemplified by "artistic puppet theatres," in which the service given to the puppet by live intermediaries or stage companions is further exploited, so that the puppet may be comprehended as being, explicitly, " 'puppetlike' . . . [with] the puppet as scenic character and as material object at the same time" (1988 [1983]: 78). Jurkowski cites a number of productions that "confront the puppet theatre with the live theatre, in order to intensify the puppet theatre's characteristics," or that allow the puppet to be "aware of the fact that it is manipulated by somebody," and to be "conscious" of being a puppet, thus stressing the puppet as a "metaphor of powerlessness and control by external forces" (1988 [1983]: 79).

It is, of course, the argument of this study that while the puppet's process of double-vision is explicitly exploited by such artistic theatres, it is implicitly exploited by every employment of the puppet. But Jurkowski is certainly correct in identifying the explicit exploitation of the two aspects of the puppet, "scenic character and material object at the same time," as being fundamental to the period McPharlin calls "the puppet revival" (1938: i).

Jurkowski concludes his history with contemporary puppetry, in which "all the elements of puppet theatre [are] atomized" (1988 [1983]: 67). By this, he means that the traditional techniques of puppet theatre, including the staging, the relationship between puppet and puppet-operator, and the presentation of puppets and actors together, are "taken to pieces," and that such theatre is "characterized by the constant pulsation of the means of expression and their relationships" (1988 [1983]: 81–82).

In this final kind of theatre, the elements of the performance are at-
omized, and none can be identified as being in the service of others.
This could be called the deconstruction of the puppet theatre, although
Jurkowski does not use that term. His example is a Polish production:

> [Josef Krofta] directed his own script after *Don Quixote* by Cervantes.
> He introduced on the stage a number of live actors and some puppets.
> The principal characters (e.g., don Quixote and Sancho Panza) were
> doubly represented by men and puppets. At one time we saw the char-
> acters represented by men, at another time by puppets, and sometimes
> by both of them. The scene of don Quixote's defeat in the inn was per-
> formed using different means of expression. One actor with a stick in
> his hand beat the bench where don Quixote was supposed to be lying;
> another actor pretending to be beaten shrieked like a madman; another
> one was damaging the puppet of don Quixote. (1988 [1983]: 67)

It might be noted that writers and artists involved with puppetry find
the story of Don Quixote to be virtually irresistible. Perhaps this is because it contains not only the wonderful incident of Don Pedro's puppet show, but also a recurrent theme of ontological paradox, such as
the windmill imagined to be a monster. Such an ontological paradox is,
as we have suggested, essential to the puppet.

Jurkowski argues that in Krofta's production, "we may find a new
combination of the means of expression, and so, to some extent, a new
system of signs," the puppetry of which must be comprehended on its
own terms (1988 [1983]: 67). But is there anything about this production, or about similarly atomized productions, that is not comprehensible through the synchronic approach of this study?

In the scene just described, Jurkowski finds significance in the atomization of the character of Don Quixote, as represented by a location on
a bench, an actor pretending to be beaten and shrieking like a madman,
and the damaging of the puppet of Don Quixote. Surely this is a complex piece of staging; but does the scene, in fact, even contain a puppet? The tortured figure of Don Quixote can scarcely be considered
one, even by Jurkowski's definition, in that it is accorded neither movement nor speech. The character of Don Quixote has certainly been atomized; but the puppet has not, in that there is no puppet. The

theatrical figure of Don Quixote seems to be nothing more than a prop, an effigy of Don Quixote, subjected to physical damage in a symbolic manner quite common to effigies. The significance of such a scene to the comprehension of the puppet seems quite limited.

Lacking familiarity with the production in question, one finds it difficult to comment on how, or even whether, puppets, or props similar to puppets, are used in other scenes. But let us imagine a scene. An actor playing Don Quixote sits in an up-stage study, reading of chivalry; he pauses to stare out toward the audience. A small puppet, also playing Don Quixote, enters down-stage right, in full knightly armor, mounted on Rocinante. As the puppet Don Quixote rides along, the actor Don Quixote sees it and follows its progress. It stops briefly, mid-stage, and the actor speaks a line of dialogue for it. When the puppet exits, down-stage left, the actor puts down his book and reaches for a knightly helmet that sits upon his desk. (This scene is suggested by one in *Don Quixote,* as adapted for the Pickwick Puppet Theatre by Ken Moses, 1980.)

In this imaginary scene, the character of Don Quixote is atomized in a manner similar to that described by Jurkowski. But in it, the down-stage representation of Don Quixote is, by all definitions, a puppet. Jurkowski is correct in arguing that the atomization of character "stress[es] . . . theatrical and metaphorical functions" (1988 [1983]: 81). But regardless of such emphasis, the puppet remains comprehensible as a puppet.

Thus concludes Jurkowski's survey of the puppet's journey through the sign systems. It is significant to note that Bunraku puppetry has no place in Jurkowski's schema, for although Bunraku "may be compared with the most advanced artistic puppet theatres of Europe and America of our time," it differs in being centuries older, and in being a closed system, while the contemporary theatre is "obviously an open system" (1988 [1983]: 65–67). This inability to encompass Bunraku arises from the schema's basis in European models, to which non-European puppetry fails, predictably enough, to conform. How seriously are we to take a diachronic approach that scarcely notices puppetry as it is practiced in three-quarters of the world?

The sign system of the puppet theatre, in Jurkowski's sense of the term, is one that, on a fundamental level, creates itself anew with each puppet tradition, perhaps even with each puppet performance, as the puppet is made to deploy an almost infinite variety of signs and combinations of signs. As Jurkowski writes: "The relations between the object (the puppet) and the power sources [the speakers and manipulators] change all the time" (1988 [1983]: 79–80). He is certainly correct that this distinguishes puppet theatre from live theatre. In the latter, the presence of the living actor restricts not only the signs that can be deployed, but also their manner of deployment; owing to that presence, it is possible to postulate certain fixed aspects of a sign system of the live theatre. But Jurkowski is incorrect in suggesting that the puppet has been employed in the service of four possible sign systems; one must say, rather, that the sign systems of the puppet theatre, in its diachronic diversity, are multitudinous, and that there is no one thing that can properly be idealized as puppet theatre. One must then examine the puppet as a unique theatrical medium, and see how it can have such a protean nature.

Contrary to Jurkowski, one can easily discuss in the same breath Bunraku puppets, Petrushka, the characters in Master Pedro's theatre, and even the character of the juggler performing its trick on some city sidewalk. In every instance, the puppet is a perceived object that, through the deployment of signs from its three sign-systems, is imagined to be alive; the ontological paradox of this double-vision creates a pleasure that accompanies any and all other pleasures afforded by the puppet.

PUPPETS, PERFORMING OBJECTS, AND ACTORS

The concept of double-vision allows us to comprehend the essential process of puppetry as a theatrical art. But of course, the puppet is only one way of presenting theatre: throughout the world, what has been called the "performing object" is also involved in theatrical presentation, and, obviously, theatre is very frequently presented by the actor. What distinguishes the puppet from the performing object and the actor? Or, to put the question another way, how does the double-vision provoked by the puppet differ from the manner in which performing objects and actors are seen by audiences?

Frank Proschan, an incisive American scholar of puppetry and folklore, places the puppet in the category of performing objects that "we invest with the powers to speak and to move" (1983: 3). He further defines performing objects as "material images of humans, animals, or spirits that are created, displayed, or manipulated in narrative or dramatic performance. While puppetry is at the center of this definition, it is not alone" (1983: 4). In an earlier article, however, Proschan locates the puppet differently within the category: "Puppets are but the extreme example of performing objects, a category of phenomena which range from dolls of children's play, through narrated scrolls and images, to peep shows and magic object, and to the costumes and props of theatrical performance (to mention only a few examples)" (1981: 554). Other examples he mentions are "dancers who wear masks," "worshippers who bear icons in a religious procession," and "storytellers who trace images in snow or sand"; all, he says, "manifest the urge to give life to nonliving things, as they animate objects in dramatic performances and use material images as surrogates for human actors" (1983: 3).

The category "performing object" is remarkably broad, and, as defined by Proschan, incorporates practices that may deserve categories of their own; all that unites them is that they make use of nonliving things that are made animate. A category as broad as this would of course include puppetry, although, as we have seen, the very terms nonliving and animate are so imprecise, if not outright incorrect, as to be of dubious value.

We must ask, however, whether the puppet is, in Proschan's terms, a central example of the performing object or an extreme one. For if it is central, then the essence of the performing object must be the essence of the puppet, while if it is extreme, then one could argue that the puppet differs enough to justify separate categorization. Answering this question requires a means of organizing the range of activity covered by the category "performing object." Unfortunately, Proschan does not offer an organizational means, and so the puppet can be central or extreme, depending on the rhetorical occasion. It will be best to analyze some of the performing objects mentioned by Proschan, to help us understand the organization of the category, and the place of the puppet within or without it.

Two types of performing objects mentioned by Proschan fall outside of the context of the theatre: "icons [borne by worshippers] in a religious procession," and "dolls of children's play." It is not, perhaps, coincidental that, as we have seen, the puppet has been explained as evolving, and as gaining its power, from the religious figure and the childhood toy. Both are, in the broadest sense, objects made to perform. But neither is used for "narrative or dramatic" purpose; or, to put it another way, neither is concerned with theatrical representation in itself. As such, perhaps Proschan should not include them, and they will not be discussed here.

Within the context of theatre are Proschan's examples of "narrated scrolls and images," which would include "storytellers who trace images in snow or sand," as well as "dancers who wear masks" and "props of theatrical performance." These three types of activity may be said to involve, respectively, objects of narration, objects of mask/costume, and objects of staging.

We have already treated objects of narration in our discussion of Jurkowski's example of Master Pedro's puppet show. These objects, be they illustrated scrolls or images traced in sand or snow, are alike in that while they can be given speech, they are not, and cannot be, given movement. Their "animation," to use Proschan's unfortunate term, is so limited that one can doubt whether they are animated at all; they are nothing more or less than pictorial illustrations, of the sort commonly found in illustrated children's books.

We also have already treated objects of mask/costume, in our discussion of whether the actor in a mask and/or costume is to be considered a puppet. We should add now that, while objects of mask/costume can be given movement, they are not, and cannot be, given speech, in that any speech associated with them is simply the speech of the actor or dancer who wears them. Again, their animation is so limited that one can wonder whether it exists at all, for the movement given them is but the performance movement of the actor or dancer who wears them, and is accorded to the performer, and not the object.

Objects of staging have not yet been treated. Proschan offers little comment on them, and no actual examples. Veltrusky, however, provides an extended discussion, and informs us that they include props and scenery, and can "be present as real objects or as signs such as wooden swords, cardboard columns, painted trees, etc." (1983: 85). According to Veltruský, objects of staging are

> animated by acting when the characters are represented treating them as live beings or when they conceal live characters. . . . In Molière's *Tartuffe* III/7, after a brief exchange with Tartuffe, Orgon runs to the door through which he drove out his son at the end of the preceding scene and addresses to the door an angry speech intended for the son. . . . In Act IV/2, Elmire and Orgon move a table to a prominent place and the man hides under it and listens to Elmire's conversation with Tartuffe in the next scene; during that conversation the actress repeatedly directs the spectators' attention to the table and the character hiding under it by producing sounds addressed to him. (1983: 86)

This involves a broad conception of animation indeed, and is only barely encompassed by Proschan's definition of "performing objects," which stipulates that such objects be "material images of humans, animals, or spirits." One might take Molière's door and table to be material images of the spirits of doors and tables, but then again, one might not: one could choose, rather, to think that the door and table have in no way been animated, and are but the props or objects they purport to be. Veltruský himself is aware of this second choice, and warns that a "broadened concept of personification may blur the distinction between puppets on the one hand and objects perceived on the stage as agents on the other" (1983: 88). The object of staging is given neither movement nor speech; although it might be moved or spoken to, it is not and cannot be accorded the pretense of moving or speaking for itself, and it is animated only by the action that takes place around it.

Thus it seems that objects of staging are at one end of the range of performing object activity, an end marked by a barely existent and highly attenuated sense of animation. Objects of narration seem to be toward the center of the range, being performing objects whose animation is somewhat existent, through the occasional imputation of speech, but is still rather tenuous. Objects of mask/costume seem to be at the other end of the range, an end marked by a more substantial sense of animation that arises from the movement they are given.

All along this range of performing object activity, however, the object itself is perceived by the audience to be an object, and, regardless of its relative level of animation, is imagined by the audience to be nothing other than an object. This should be clear even with objects of mask/costume: a mask or costume is nothing more than an object worn by a living being, be this person an actor or a dancer; life is not imagined to inhere in the mask or costume itself, but in the living being who wears it.

Beyond the extreme end of this range of performing objects, provoking double-vision in the mind of its audience, comes the puppet: like the performing object, it is perceived to be an object, but, unlike the performing object, it is imagined to have life. In this way it essentially differs. A case in point would be Jurkowski's example of the Polish *Don Quixote* production. The effigy of the unfortunate knight that is beaten by an actor is a performing object of staging, perceived and imagined to be nothing other than an object, but given a tenuous animation by the action around it. If it were to be truly animated, or, more precisely, if it were to be given movement and speech so that the audience would imagine it to have a life of its own, only then would it be a puppet. The puppet is, of course, a performing object as Proschan defines performing objects, but the concept of double-vision allows us to recognize that the definition can only in its broadest sense include the puppet.

Just as the puppet has been located within the range of the performing object, so has it also been located in what may be called the range of the actor. As we have seen, McPharlin suggests that the puppet is seen by its audience in the same manner as is the actor: "When they become alive in their theatre, the overwhelming appeal is that of the theatre only" (1938: 1). Batchelder states plainly that "the puppet is an actor participating in some kind of theatrical performance" (1947: xv). But while the puppet's location in the range of performing object activity required some discussion before being identified as essentially beyond that range, its location in the range of acting activity does not seem to be in doubt. Even McPharlin and Batchelder would agree that the puppet differs in some essential manner from the live actor.

The actor has been the subject of vast scholarship, much of it contentious; the plenitude of theory concerning live acting more than compensates for the scarcity concerning the performing object. It will be impossible to offer here anything but the briefest discussion of acting, which must rely, to a great degree, either on the reader's knowledge of the scholarship, or on his or her lack of interest in it.

Having offered that caveat, we may note, as we did with performing objects, three points along the range of acting technique: at one extreme, naturalistic acting; toward the center of the range, presentational acting; and at the other extreme, mask or costume acting. These terms will be clarified with some description and examples.

In naturalistic acting, the actor's own personality and status as actor are submerged beneath the character he or she represents; the actor, to the greatest degree possible, desires to be acknowledged by the audience only as that character. The semiotician Keir Elam refers to such acting as "illusionistic," with "mimetic principles 'authenticating' the representation" (1980: 59). Such acting is frequently associated with the Russian director Stanislavsky, and has been the dominant style of acting in the twentieth century. It relies on the single and surprisingly pervasive convention that the audience will simply acknowledge what it sees on-stage to be a representation of stark reality.

In presentational acting, the actor's own personality and status as actor are not fully submerged; to a greater or lesser degree, the actor desires to be acknowledged not only as the character he or she represents, but also as an individual and/or as an actor. Elam describes the "conventions of direct address" and "meta-theatrical reference" in this type of acting, in which the "breaking of the mimetic illusion" is a more or less frequent occurrence (1980: 59). Bertolt Brecht is, perhaps, the most familiar exponent of such acting, and his famous V-Effect, termed in English either alienation or estrangement, is central to it, keeping the audience from too close an identification with the actor's dramatic character. In fact, presentational acting has a long and varied history: James Brandon informs us that, in Japan, "it is part of the 'game' of Kabuki for the spectator to see the actor-as-actor as well as the character in a drama" (Brandon 1975: 42). The basis of presentational acting, wherever it is favored, is in the stage convention of "reality" being intentionally supplemented with other conventions that undermine it.

In mask/costume acting, the actor neither makes a pretense of being a naturalistic dramatic character, nor desires to be acknowledged as a person or as an actor who happens to be playing a role. Rather, as Malkin writes, "something is interposed between [the actor] and the audience [that] partakes of mystery, ritual, symbol, and the intellect" (1975: 7). Although the actor is most certainly alive, the performance is transformed by the mask/costume object he or she wears. We can again make use of our mundane example of Mickey Mouse cavorting in Disneyland: no doubt we are in the presence of an actor of an extreme type, who, if not quite partaking of mystery, ritual, and so on, nonetheless performs through the transforming mediation of the mask and costume.

All along this range of acting technique, regardless of metatheatrical conventions and mask/costume interpositions, the actor is perceived by the audience to be nothing other than alive; the actor is also imagined to be alive, although the imaginary life is not usually that of the actor, but of the character he or she is representing. This should be clear even with mask/costume acting: the actor in the mask or costume is perceived and imagined to have real life, while the mask or costume is obviously an object under his or her direct control. The object nature of the mask/costume is not perceived to inhere in the living being who wears it, but in the mask/costume itself.

Beyond the extreme end of the range of the live actor, provoking double-vision in the mind of its audience, comes the puppet: like the actor, it is imagined to be alive, but, unlike the actor, it is perceived to be an object. In this way the puppet essentially differs from the actor.

The puppet and the actor have the same three sign-systems at their disposal, and it might seem that the audience would thus acknowledge them in the same manner. Bogatyrev points out, however, that "despite the fact that an actor expresses regal dignity by his costume, the sign of age in his gait, the sign that he represents a foreigner by his speech, and so on, we still see him not only as a system of signs but also as a living person" (1976 [1938]: 48). Beneath the signs deployed by the actor, the audience cannot help but see the living being. Veltruský writes:

> The actor's body . . . enters into the dramatic situation with all of its
> properties. A living human being can understandably not take off some

of them and keep on only those he needs for a given situation. . . . This
is what makes the figure of the actor more complex and richer, we are
tempted to say more concrete, as compared to other sign carriers. (1964
[1940]: 84–85)

The living being of the actor complicates the artificiality of his or her
deployed signs of character with the simultaneous deployment of signs
of real life. But the puppet has no real life. Strip the actor and the puppet of their theatrical signs, and you still have a living person, while the
puppet has ceased to exist. Alexandre Bakshy, an early twentieth-century American writer, expresses this difference with a satisfying apho-
rism: "We can never apply the same standards to the man and the
puppet. . . . The puppet can never live unless it acts. The man can
never act unless he lives" (quoted in Batchelder 1947: 287).

The distinction between the actor and the puppet, between the person perceived to be alive and the puppet perceived to be an object, has
significant theatrical ramifications. Obraztsov writes that "the puppet
is not a man, it is an allegory of man. Like all allegories, it has the
power of generalizing reality" (1967 [1965]: 20). Maeterlinck makes
much the same point, in his own characteristic way: "A man can speak
in his own name only; he has no right to speak in the name of the
whole world of the dead" (quoted in Jurkowski 1988 [1979]: 12–13).
The puppet, however, has that right, as it is not encumbered with a
real life of its own. It may speak in the name of any man or number of
men. As Kleist suggests, "grace appears most purely in that human
form which either has no consciousness or an infinite consciousness;
that is, in the puppet or in the god" (1978 [1810]: 1212). Because the
only consciousness the puppet can have is that consciousness invested in
it by an anonymous and potentially infinite audience, it may be imagined to bear the consciousness of an anonymous and infinite world.

The relationships between the puppet and the performing object,
and between the puppet and the actor, can be defined clearly: the puppet is just beyond the extreme ends of the ranges of both performing
object and acting. Although the puppet can be construed to be within
either range, depending on the definitions offered, the concept of double-vision clarifies it as being a distinct phenomenon in its own right.

Nearest to the puppet within each range are the performing object of mask or costume on the one side, and the actor in a mask or costume on the other. Earlier, we discussed the attempt by those involved in puppetry to annex the mask; owing to the proximate relations of the puppet and the mask, this should not be surprising. Neither should it be surprising if scholars and practitioners in the field of masking were to attempt to annex the puppet. As we have seen, however, the puppet essentially differs from the mask/costume performing object and the actor who wears a mask or costume, and comprehension of the puppet requires that it be considered as a distinct, if related, phenomenon.

It will perhaps be useful to present schematically the relationships just discussed:

Performing Objects	Puppets	Actors
Staging		Mask/Costume
Narration	Puppets	Presentational
Mask/Costume		Naturalistic
Perceived: Object	Perceived: Object	Perceived: Life
Imagined: Object	Imagined: Life	Imagined: Life

Julie Taymor, a contemporary American theatre-artist who brilliantly mixes each of the media discussed above, most especially in her production *Juan Darien,* justifies such usage by explaining that "the change of scale, the mixture of media — live actors, next to masked actors, next to puppets — helps you move through different levels of reality" (1983: 114).

The flavor of *Juan Darien* is captured by Stephen Kaplin, an American scholar and puppet-artist who helped build, and performed in, the production:

In one powerful scene, Juan, a young boy who was originally an orphaned tiger cub, saved from the hunter's gun by a mother's pity, witnesses the death of his adopted mother. At the start of the scene, Juan is played by a Bunraku puppet; but at the moment of his mother's death, the Juan puppet is replaced by an unmasked boy actor. The dying mother, played by a masked actress, sits up in her bed and reaches out to the boy. He takes her masked face in his hands. She falls back, dead, leaving the empty mask in his hands. After a sorrowful duet from the Latin Requiem, Juan climbs to the top of [a] miniature village . . . and buries the mother's mask next to [a] toy-sized church. (1989: 48)

There is a compelling poetry to the movement between "different levels of reality" in this scene. Kaplin notes that "the young boy's anguish at the death of the only human that has shown him love humanizes him. This inner transformation is indicated metaphorically by transferring the Juan role from puppet to human" (1989: 48–49). Equally significant is the moment of the mother's death, which turns on the removal of her mask, the symbol of her persona.

The mixture of media not only allows Taymor to relate a magical-realistic tale in the recent Latin American style, but also allows her to make telling theatrical points about the nature of humanity. By employing the "change of scale" between performing objects, actors, and puppets, she enables each medium to challenge and enrich the others, and compels the audience to confront conflicting ideas about what is an "object," and what a "life." Distinguishing the puppet from the performing object and the actor on the basis of the double-vision it provokes does not isolate the puppet from them, but, rather, explains the relationships between the three media, and clarifies the way in which they can interact.

II

DESCRIBING THE PUPPET

4

STANDARD DESCRIPTIONS

When people talk about puppets, whether or not they can articulate precisely what a puppet is, and whether or not they are interested in explaining the nature of the puppet's appeal, they use particular terms to describe how one puppet or puppet-show is similar to another, and different from yet others; after all, every work of art exists within the general context of its art, and meaningful appreciation of a work requires some understanding of its relationship to that context. But what are the terms used to make distinctions among works of puppet art, and how do these distinctions shape discussion about puppetry? The basis of description is a vocabulary that can be used to compare and contrast. Unfortunately, the descriptive vocabulary for the puppet is limited and confusing.

The simplest method of description involves little more than an efflorescence of adjectives applied to specific puppets or puppet-shows: this puppet is small, that one large; this show is colorful, that one theatrically complex. Examples of this method are legion. Here is one from the Russian artist Nina Efimova, offered with an awareness that her contributions to the art are not, essentially, scholarly: "The gypsy girl moves majestically. Her radiant face is white, utterly without color. The hair is made from frayed rope, dipped into black paint and curled into ringlets. The soft dress is of fustian dyed canary-yellow and of lilac muslin" (1935: 149).

This description contains detailed and useful information for the reader's re-creation of a particular puppet; it is, however, of limited use for comparing and contrasting this puppet with others, unless, of course, the effect of frayed rope, as opposed to that of rope that has not been frayed, is at issue. This method of description is limited in that, however much information it may purvey, its vocabulary is not especially suited for comparing and contrasting. It is not concerned with what may be called systems of description; that is, with taxonomic descriptions that allow for the comparing and contrasting of puppets. Yet such systems, such taxonomies, would seem to offer the best chance for the development of a useful vocabulary.

Taxonomy is a misunderstood science. As Stephen Jay Gould, professor of biology and geology at Harvard University, explains in his book *Wonderful Life*:

> Taxonomy (the science of classification) is often undervalued as a glorious form of filing—with each species in its folder, like a stamp in its prescribed place in an album; but taxonomy is a fundamental and dynamic science, dedicated to exploring the causes of relationships and similarities among organisms. Classifications are theories about the basis of natural order, not dull categories compiled only to avoid chaos. (1989: 98)

Of course, our study is not concerned with the natural order of organisms, as is Gould's when he discusses the taxonomy of Precambrian fauna. Nonetheless, the principles of "the science of classification" are of significance to the study of puppetry, as they are to the study of all arts, for the problem of describing "relationships and similarities" requires taxonomic theory. And, as Gould suggests throughout his book, taxonomies, and the theories that are imbedded in them, powerfully shape the way people comprehend and discuss their subjects.

The simple method of description taken from Efimova seems predicated on the theory that each puppet is unique. This is certainly true, but only in a literal sense. Despite such uniqueness, each puppet is in some way like and unlike other puppets, and we will understand more about the unique value of each puppet if we understand its place in the general world of puppets.

Puppetry, as we have noted previously, and as every writer on puppet theatre is compelled to note, has traditional roots in many cultures. Perhaps this is why one of the two predominant methods of taxonomy uses the variety of puppet traditions as its organizing principle. This method is diachronic in approach, and may be called the historic-geographic method.

Bil Baird's expansive book *The Art of the Puppet* employs this method. It is not only one of the best-selling books on puppetry ever published, but is also an insightful and delightful overview of the phenomenon of the puppet. An examination of the book's table of contents makes plain the basic principles of the historic-geographic method: Chapter 3, "Eastern Heritage," deals with puppet traditions of India and Indonesia; Chapter 4, "Angels, Devils & Everyman," deals with those of northern and eastern Europe; Chapter 5, "Karaghioz: A Turkish Delight," with those of southeastern Europe. The next three chapters deal with traditions of, respectively, England, Italy, and "the Orient," meaning China and Japan; the final three chapters relate the history of Western puppetry in, respectively, the late eighteenth and early nineteenth centuries, the late nineteenth and early twentieth centuries, and the mid-twentieth century (1965: 5).

The Art of the Puppet demonstrates the organizational value of the historic-geographic method, especially for a popular work. Such value, however, does not reside in the taxonomy presented, for this system has two significant problems, one practical, the other theoretical.

The practical problem is that the historic-geographic method breaks down upon close examination of the history and geography involved. The historic periods that Baird postulates are little more than artificial constructs. In fact, he seems interested in historical change only when discussing Western Europe; he is generally silent about change over time in Eastern cultures, perhaps on the assumption that Western readers are not interested in such matters, or perhaps on the facile presumption that the Orient is timeless. But even within his discussion of Western traditions, his sense of history seems quite arbitrary.

To take one example: Baird's chapter on the eighteenth and early nineteenth centuries is entitled "The Impact of Genius," and discusses the role in Western puppetry of such luminaries as Gluck, Gozzi, Seraphin, Sand, and Bizet. But the temporal proximity of these people in

no way suggests any unity of thought toward the puppet among them
or during this period, whatever broader cultural movements might
have been afoot. Baird is engaging in nothing more than a glorified
form of name-dropping to advance the argument that at last puppetry
was being taken seriously. But, as Baird is aware, these people formed
no particular school of thought concerning the puppet, and had little
impact on the course of European puppetry. Indeed, even as individ-
uals, their involvement with puppetry tended to be incidental and superficial. George Sand's actual involvement with puppetry was limited
to sewing costumes for her son's puppets, and composing some accounts of his theatrical efforts. Of Sand, Edward Gordon Craig writes
that "the dignity or the profundity of puppets is lost on her" (quoted in
McPharlin 1938: 14). McPharlin comments, in the same vein, that
Sand lacked any "insight into the puppet's aesthetic" (1938: 14). And
of all the famous personages cited by Baird, Sand was perhaps the most
concerned with puppetry.

The geographic areas that Baird postulates are even more problematic, both for what they include and what they exclude. Again, one
example: Baird's joining together the many traditions of Indian puppet
theatre is, at the least, bold; when he lumps with them the many puppet traditions of Indonesia, he becomes foolhardy. He discusses these
traditions together because they are, in a broad sense, geographically
proximate, and because most of them have been influenced by Hindu
literature; but as Baird himself suggests, the relationships between the
various traditions in India alone are quite unclear (1965: 46–60). Moreover, the relationship of any Indian tradition to the various traditions of
Indonesia is the subject of substantial controversy. As Brandon reports,
"the Indian origin of Wajang theory [that is, of Javanese puppets] has
been widely debated, with inconclusive results" (1970: 3).

And then there is the matter of what must be excluded. Again, to
take a single example: between the geographic borders of Baird's chapters on "Eastern Heritage" (India and Indonesia) and "Oriental Tradition" (China and Japan) are located fascinating puppet traditions that
cannot be incorporated in either chapter, because the traditions are simply too different. The Thai tradition of *Nang yai* uses shadow puppets
as large as seven feet high and four feet wide, usually manipulated in

front of the shadow screen; the Burmese tradition of *Yoke thay* uses marionettes controlled with up to sixty strings, relating stories based on Buddhist lore and Burmese history; the Vietnamese tradition of water-puppets uses figures operated by long bamboo rods and extravagant contrivances of strings, that perform on a rising stage, amidst bursting firecrackers, in the middle of a lake (Malkin 1977: 120–33).

The geographic areas that Baird terms the East and the Orient exemplify the practical troubles of the historic-geographic method: each includes traditions that are relatively independent, while together they exclude traditions that are significant in their own right.

There does not seem to be any immediate solution to this practical problem of history and geography. While Baird's oversimplifications are unfortunate, a thorough classification of puppets on the basis of history and geography seems not yet possible, owing in part to a dearth of accounts relating the details of any number of puppet traditions. Baird's bibliography contains but a handful of works devoted to non-Western puppetry (1965: 249); Malkin's informative *Traditional and Folk Puppets of the World* offers only a dozen or so additional non-Western sources, (1977: 187–91). The problem is not so much with the research of Baird and Malkin, who have gleaned what information they could from accessible published sources; rather, it is with the paucity of such sources. Until additional studies are undertaken, the historic-geographic method must, of necessity, resort to artificial historic and geographic boundaries.

The theoretical problem with the historic-geographic method is that if every manifestation of puppetry is to be viewed primarily within the context of its historic-geographic tradition, then the puppets themselves cannot easily be considered outside of their traditional contexts. Or, to put it another way, the historic-geographic method makes little allowance for comparison between puppets of differing traditions. Again, to take one example: the Karaghioz tradition, found in Greece and derived from Turkish performance, uses what are generally known as shadow-puppets; so do a number of traditions in India and Indonesia; so does a particular tradition in China; and then there are contemporary shadow-puppets in Europe and America. In what ways are these various shadow-puppets alike, and in what ways different? The historic-geographic method obscures the obvious similarities by focusing attention on the obvious differences of history and geography. But might not an examination of their similarities shed light not only on shadow-puppets in general, but on the choices behind, and the implications of, the traditions themselves?

In fact, Baird offers a brief comparison of a few of these shadow-puppet traditions, noting that the manner in which the control-rod is connected to the shadow-puppet differs among them, thus enabling different movements for the puppets (1965: 79). This is, however, one of the rare instances of such comparison in his book. It is revealing that the comparison itself must rely upon the taxonomic method soon to be discussed, as the historic-geographic method lacks the vocabulary for comparing and contrasting.

It might seem unfair to apply criticism of this sort to a popular work such as Baird's. It should be said, though, that popular works are nearly the only works on puppetry available in the English language, and that such works embody the discussion that has preceded them, and shape the discussion that will follow. For these reasons, such criticism seems not only fair, but necessary. The two basic problems identified in Baird's book might be noted in any general study that follows the historic-geographic method.

It should be reiterated, however, that the historic-geographic method has ample value when writers maintain their focus on a particular historic-geographic area. Works such as Brandon's *On Thrones of Gold: Three Javanese Shadow Plays,* Speaight's *History of the English Puppet Theatre,* Adachi's *Backstage at Bunraku,* Stalberg's *China's Puppets,* and Linda Myrsiades's *The Karagiozis Heroic Performance in Greek Shadow Theatre* are invaluable guides to the traditions they examine. When a score of additional such works, treating of other traditions, can be cited, the historic-geographic method might at last provide grounds, given an adequate vocabulary, for a thorough diachronic aesthetics of the puppet.

This study has regularly used descriptive terms that have their basis in another taxonomic method, one that currently dominates English language discussion of the puppet; indeed, the terms are regularly employed even in historic-geographic writing, as we have noted in Baird's work. The method from which these terms derive has so profoundly shaped discussion of the puppet that even to speak of it as one method among others might seem striking. This method, which generally, though not exclusively, takes a synchronic approach, follows from the observation that the puppet is a physical construct that must be manipulated, and may be called the object-control method.

This method of taxonomic classification begins with a fundamental division. As Cyril Beaumont, a mid-twentieth-century English puppet-artist, puts it: "All puppets fall into two main groups: round or three-dimensional puppets, and flat or two-dimensional puppets" (1958: 17). This division is based on what would seem to be the most obvious of criteria for classifying puppets as objects, and is observed, either explicitly or implicitly, by most writers who discuss the subject in any formal way (see Blackham 1948: 1–5; Veltruský 1983: 69; McPharlin 1938: 85–92; Arnott 1964: 58–65).

Beyond this fundamental division, the object-control method organizes puppets according to certain types, predicated on their manner of control. The following is Beaumont's version of this taxonomy (1958: 17):

Flat [Two-dimensional]	**Round** [Three-dimensional]
1. Paper or board puppets	1. String puppets, or marionettes
2. Shadow puppets	2. Rod-puppets
	3. Jigging-puppets
	4. Glove-puppets or hand-puppets
	5. Magnetically controlled puppets
	6. Japanese three-man puppets

Most of these terms will be familiar; a few may seem idiosyncratic. The familiarities and idiosyncrasies will be pointed up by a look at other object-control taxonomies.

Olive Blackham, a mid-century English puppet-artist and writer, offers the following classification of puppets, here given in summary form (1948: 1–5):

Flat [Two-dimensional]

1. Puppets of Which the Substance Is Seen (e.g. "the Toy Theatre")
2. Puppets of Which Only the Shadow Is Seen (e.g. "shadow figures")
   a. "opaque" figures casting a "black shadow"
   b. "translucent and colored" figures casting a "colored shadow"

Round [Three-dimensional]

1. Puppets Worked from Above by Means of Strings (e.g. conventional marionettes)
2. Puppets Worked from Above by Means of Rods (e.g. "the puppets of Liège" and "of Sicily")
3. Puppets Worked from Below by Means of Rods (e.g. conventional rod-puppets)
4. Puppets Worked from Below by Means of Cords, Pulleys, and Other Devices (e.g. "the large Japanese puppets"; presumably, Bunraku puppets)
5. Puppets Worked on the Hand from Below (e.g. glove-puppets or hand-puppets)

Blackham's terminology is rather clumsy, but the clumsiness arises in part from her desire to provide some systematic logic. Distinctions are made between possible locations of the puppet-operator (above or below the puppet), and between actual means of puppet control (strings, rods, etc.). The effort is well-intentioned, but for reasons that will become clear, it remains insufficient.

In his thesis, "Aesthetic of the Puppet Revival," McPharlin does not chart out a formal taxonomy; nonetheless, a taxonomy is implicit in the work, and he makes reference to marionettes, hand-puppets, and "the other five principal types of puppets" (1938: 33). When he reviews them, however, he discusses a total of only six types. They are, in his order of discussion (1938: 85–92):

1. String-puppets
2. Stick or rod-puppets
3. Jigging-puppets
4. Hand-puppets

5. Paper or board puppets

6. Shadow-figures

Elsewhere in his thesis, McPharlin makes brief mention of Bunraku puppets, "four-foot-tall puppets of such mechanical elaboration that they may raise their eyebrows and clench their fists" (1938: 56); as he makes no mention of the rod-puppet/marionettes of Liège and Sicily, one may assume he considers the Bunraku puppet as his seventh type.

Arnott is satisfied to enumerate "four main types of puppets" (1964: 58). They are, in his order of discussion (1964: 58–65):

1. Glove-puppets

2. Shadow-puppets

3. Rod-puppets

4. Marionettes

No doubt these are the terms that have been most familiar throughout this review of object-control taxonomies. And yet all of the terms used by these writers are worthy of consideration, for the most idiosyncratic tell as much about this method as the familiar.

Following Beaumont's taxonomy, the first type is that of flat "paper or board puppets," also mentioned by Blackham and McPharlin. According to Beaumont, the most famous of these are "associated with the Juvenile Drama, that robust lively toy theatre of the second half of the nineteenth century, in which youthful producers acquired their actors from the 'penny plain and twopence coloured' sheets" (1958: 19). Blackham suggests that this type is "in origin a toy for children" (1948: 1). McPharlin dispenses with it quickly, stating that "it is too restricted in movement to give much scope to the artist; and when he plays with them, he is apt to spend more energy on the scenic panoply than on the figures themselves" (1938: 91).

Gunther Böhmer, a contemporary German scholar, notes:

[Such] theatre imbued the filigreed magnificence of [the diorama] with an illusion of life. Since it has moveable figures, which can be slid here and there by means of wires and sticks or even magnets, the paper the-

atre is counted among the many forms of puppetry. Fundamentally it is
closely associated with the "live" theatre, which, in complete contrast
to the intentions of puppetry, it seeks to imitate as closely and with as
much authenticity as possible. (1971 [1969]: 53)

Following Böhmer, and according to all of the definitions discussed earlier, the toy theatre is not, strictly speaking, puppetry at all: its imitation is not so much of dramatic action as it is of the live theatre's
grandeur and glamour. This is not to suggest that the toy theatre cannot be used as puppetry, but only to recognize that generally it is not so
used. Although a fascinating phenomenon in its own right, it would
seem more appropriately studied from perspectives other than that of
puppet aesthetics.

Lost in the many references to the toy theatre are two related types
of puppets that may fairly be characterized, using Blackham's terms, as
"flat" puppets "of which the substance is seen." Although they have no
generally accepted names, they may be called cut-out puppets and
panel-puppets.

The cut-out puppet is nothing more than its name suggests: the outline of a figure is cut from some material such as cardboard or wood
and given a coat of paint or costume. Bob Brown's production of *The
Enchanted Child,* our American example in the introduction, makes effective use of such cut-out puppets for minor characters who are perceived by the main character to be stiff and unlifelike; they are moved as
units or given one or two joints to allow them moveable arms as well.
All movement is given via rods, by the operator who supports the cut-
out. Although their movement possibilities are somewhat limited,
their design and their speech, along with such movement as they have,
allow the audience to imagine them as having life.

The panel-puppet is a bit more complex. In the Budapest State Puppet Theatre's production of Kodály's *Háry János,* many of the figures
are, in the words of György Kroó, a member of the company, "one-
dimensional figures . . . [that are] moveable and could on occasion be
used as screens" (1978: 54). By one-dimensional, Kroó means that the
puppets present only one aspect to the audience. While the cut-out
puppet separates the figure of the character from its original panel of

cardboard or wood, the panel-puppet remains essentially a freestanding unit of wall-panel. Its movement might be supplied in two ways: the unit with the figure might have one or two moveable aspects, such as a cloth sleeve into which the operator can place and move his or her arm, or a mechanical device that enables the puppet's features, such as mouth and eyes, to open and close. The entire unit can be wheeled to various locations around the stage. It is this second kind of movement that allows these puppets to be used as screens, as any unit of wall-panel might be used.

Cut-out puppets and panel-puppets, excepting their usage for the creation of shadows, seem not to have been regularly employed in any major tradition. Nonetheless, by every definition of the puppet previously discussed, these are puppets, although unnoticed by object-control taxonomers.

Next on Beaumont's list of puppet types come shadow-puppets, which have a place on all of our lists. Shadow-puppets are, essentially, nothing more than cut-out puppets, usually controlled via rods. The list-makers note, with Blackham, that their shadows can be black or colored, depending on the transparency of their materials. McPharlin comments that they, like the toy theatre, "might be considered restricted in movement were it not for their fascination . . . : a light shines through the screen, and the screen is always in a dark room. We turn toward the light as surely as sunflowers. . . . [Shadow-puppets] never give the illusion of actual life. They create a realm of fantasy with which we, reality, are permitted to merge" (1938: 91–92). It is only a quibble to point out that shadow-shows such as our Javanese example take place not in a dark room, but outdoors in the dark of night. McPharlin's point is that the shadow-puppet fascinates because the shadow is a fantastic presence upon a screen suffused with light; the shadow is uniquely free from lifelike imitation, in that it has but two dimensions.

It is not a quibble, however, to note that neither McPharlin nor any of our other list-makers acknowledge that in many shadow traditions, some of the audience, if not all, frequently, if not always, views the puppet itself, and not the puppet's shadow. The *Nang yai* tradition of Thailand, in which most of the performance takes place in front of the shadow-screen, has already been mentioned; it will also be recalled that in our Javanese example, the audience regularly sits on both sides of the screen.

Jiří Veltruský, a scholar associated with the Prague Linguistic Circle, acknowledges that sometimes the shadow-puppet itself is viewed; but despite this acknowledgment, he would banish the shadow-puppet from the realm of puppetry. As he writes in his essay "Puppetry and Acting":

> This article deals only with puppets properly so called, that is, three-dimensional puppets. . . . The shadow theatre has been left aside . . . [for although in Java people sometimes watch the puppet], there is no doubt that in the shadow theatre in general it is the shadow projected on the screen, not the object itself as in the puppet theatre, that focuses the attention. In [Charles] Magnin's felicitous formulation [1862: 181], the shadow theatre is not in the nature of mobile sculpture, as the puppet theatre is, but of mobile painting. (1983: 69)

The very qualities that, in McPharlin's estimation, make the shadow-puppet unique, render it, according to Veltruský and Magnin, not a puppet at all. How is one to resolve whether the shadow-puppet is or is not a puppet?

One might begin by noting a fundamental error of perception committed by both McPharlin and Veltruský: although the shadow projected upon the screen is, indeed, two-dimensional, the puppet that casts the shadow is not. Despite the convention of classifying puppets as two- or three-dimensional, it is obvious that no physical object can have only two dimensions. Although the shadow-puppet's third dimension, that of depth, is quite insubstantial, it nonetheless exists. Indeed, the same holds true for cut-out puppets and panel-puppets as well: all are physical objects, and all have a certain amount of depth. Contrary to the fundamental division of the object-control taxonomy, there is no such thing as a two-dimensional puppet, and the shadow-puppet is as much an "object" as any other puppet.

One might continue by noting that, even if the audience were never to view the puppet directly, the viewed shadow is the creation of the puppet interposed between the shadow-screen and the light source. In

Javanese shadow-theatre, the puppet, generally moved parallel to the screen, may also be moved between the screen and the light source, causing the shadow to grow larger and diffuse, or smaller and well defined. It may also be pivoted against the screen to face in the other direction, causing its shadow to diminish to a mere line before filling out again. More rarely, the light source may be given motion, with the puppet remaining stationary, causing the shadow both to change shape and to move across the screen (Brandon 1970: 35). Whatever the mode of movement, the shadow on the screen is merely the result; the cause involves the puppet. The shadow-theatre is not "mobile painting," as Magnin and Veltruský would have it, but is as much "mobile sculpture" as any puppetry; its mobility, uniquely among puppets, is generally employed for the creation of shadows.

One might conclude, following this analysis, by noting that McPharlin and Veltruský commit an error of analysis by attending only to the shadow of the shadow-puppet. As Veltruský himself admits, in some traditions it is the puppet itself that is watched. But even when it is not, the physical object of the puppet behind the screen is the cause of the shadow and its movement, and the audience is always aware of this fact. The shadow-puppet is in every way an "object" that is given imaginary life, even if it is the shadow that garners the most attention.

It must be remarked, however, that this conclusion, however valid in a theoretical sense, runs counter to the linguistic traditions of a number of cultures; the division of puppets into two- and three-dimensional classes is not merely a Western prejudice. As Roberta Stalberg, a contemporary American scholar of Chinese culture, informs us:

> The general term for shadow theatre in China today is *pi-ying xi* or "theatre of leather shadows" because the figures are made from leather, but early on, the most widespread term for this form was *deng-ying xi,* "theatre of lantern shadows." Shadow figures have never been termed *mu-ou,* or puppet, because the Chinese have always drawn a distinction between such two-dimensional figures and three-dimensional puppets. (1984: 86)

There can be no doubt that shadow-theatre has its own distinctive history, in China as elsewhere. Nonetheless, it is worth noting that

Stalberg does not hesitate to discuss these two-dimensional figures in a book dedicated to the general study of Chinese puppetry, and that linguistic traditions such as the one in China might well be based on historical or sociological circumstances, related to the development of shadow-theatre in any given culture. Despite linguistic traditions, shadow-theatre employs "objects" that, perforce, have three dimensions, and that are intended, as are all puppets, to foster the idea of "life."

Beaumont next proceeds to "round, or three-dimensional" puppets, beginning with "string-puppets, or marionettes." These, he says, "attempt to imitate all of the movements of a human being, of which, in general, they are representations in miniature" (1958: 17). The first statement is, one hopes, an exaggeration: why use a puppet at all, when humans can far better imitate human actions? In the Indian example given in the introduction, marionettes of a simple form are employed. Each has but two strings: one from the puppet's head to the operator's hand and back down to the puppet's waist, the other from one of the puppet's hands to the operator's and then to the puppet's other hand. Such a puppet, though capable of more subtle movement than might be thought, cannot be claimed to imitate anything near "all of the movements of a human being." Beaumont's point, most likely, is that marionettes generally have bodies with four moveable limbs, whereas many other types do not. Arnott suggests, for this reason, that they are the "most generally satisfactory" of puppets (1964: 60); and the marionette has its place on every list of puppet types that employs the object-control method.

But what is the distinguishing feature of marionettes? Arnott, in defining them, calls them "jointed figures controlled from above by strings or wires" (1964: 60). Is the distinguishing feature the control from above, or is it the use of strings or wires? It will be recalled that Blackham's list distinguishes between "puppets worked from above by means of strings" and those "worked from above by means of rods." This distinction is important, because the movement possibilities created by the different means of control are not at all the same.

McPharlin writes that the "string-puppet is well able to mimic in a broad fashion almost all sorts of realistic motion. Critics who complain of its stilted walk may have been unfortunate in seeing only badly made or manipulated figures" (1938: 85). He also remarks that "in the field of non-realism . . . the string-puppet excels. . . . It is, by virtue of its strings, independent of gravity" (1938: 86). Harro Siegel, a contemporary German puppet-artist, specifies "the dream-like, floating, submissive quality of the marionette" (1967 [1965]: 21). Note, however, that McPharlin is careful to use the word string-puppet; for this dreamlike quality, as well as this "realistic motion," is beyond the capacity of the marionette controlled by an overhead rod.

Joan Gross tells us that in the Liège tradition of marionettes, "the only instrument of direct control is a single steel rod which is attached to a ring at the top of the head. This means that the puppets move in a very stiff, un-humanlike manner" (1987: 107). And, as Baird says of Sicilian marionettes:

> Their carriage is erect and movement is controlled only through the impetus of the iron rod, which lifts or twists the body at the neck. The swinging body motion also governs the stiff-legged stride. . . . The [puppet] swings a leg backward to gain momentum and then, with a twist of the body, marches forward with a thump. (1965: 120)

If the distinguishing feature of the marionette is its control from above, then the movement possibilities of the type cannot be generalized, and to classify a puppet as a marionette is to describe less than one might think. If the distinguishing feature is its use of strings, then a separate type must be set forth, as it is by Blackham, to account for the Liège and Sicilian marionettes, among yet others that are operated by rods.

The point here is that even the puppet type placed at the pinnacle of puppetry by many object-control taxonomists is not, in fact, a single and discrete type of puppet; the confusion to be found within the classification "marionette" is indicative of that to be found in most of the object-control classifications.

Next on Beaumont's list come rod-puppets, the distinguishing feature of which, as Blackham explains it, is their operation, from beneath, via rods; these puppets are also included on all of our object-control lists. Our Nigerian performance provides a good exam-

ple: these puppets have two internal rods, one providing general support, the other providing movement of the mouth; they may have
additional rods for moveable hands or legs (Böhmer 1971 [1969]: 108).
The number and function of rods vary considerably in different traditions, and often allow for remarkable nuance of movement.

Batchelder, in her massive study *Rod-Puppets and the Human Theatre,*
writes that "the rod-puppet [is] a figure worked from below the stage
floor by means of (1) rods, (2) rods and strings, or (3) hands and rods,
so that carefully controlled movement can be obtained" (1947: xix).
The "carefully controlled movement" available to the rod-puppet is
noted by all of our writers. Arnott suggests that "absolute precision of
control is possible," and that "these figures have great dignity and
beauty" (1964: 59). Many scholars and practitioners agree with
Böhmer that "the rod-puppet occupies a place between the hand-puppet and the marionette. While it has much of the directness and vitality
of the one, it also has the complicated charm and subtle individuality of
the other" (1971 [1969]: 37).

The most interesting aspect of Batchelder's definition is how inclu-
sive it is. This inclusiveness exposes, yet again, the problems of the object-control method: how broad a range of puppets is to be subsumed
under a given type, and what is the relationship of puppets across that
range?

Batchelder writes that puppets controlled "by hands and rods" are to
be considered rod-puppets. The distinguishing characteristic of Jim
Henson's Muppets is the operating mouth of each figure. Kermit the
Frog is a good example: the operator's hand goes up through a cloth
and foam body into a cloth head with a hinged mouth. By opening and
closing his or her hand, and by tilting it in various ways, the operator
opens and closes the puppet's mouth, and gives its head expressive
movement. The operator's second hand controls two rods, each of
which is attached to one of the puppet's hands, giving motion to the
arms of the puppet, which are appended to the shoulders (Henson Associates 1980: 16). According to Batchelder's definition, Kermit would
have to be called a rod-puppet. Certainly its arms are operated with
rods in a manner appropriate to this type; but, in fact, it would seem to
be its operative mouth, intimately controlled by its operator's hand,
that is its distinguishing characteristic.

Where in this taxonomy are we to place a puppet such as Kermit? And how are we to classify a puppet with an operative mouth, but with arms that are sleeves and gloves into which the operator, and sometimes an assistant, place arms and hands, as with many other Muppets? Or again, with an operative mouth, but with no arms at all, such as Ollie, of Burr Tillstrom's "Kukla, Fran, and Ollie"? Or yet again, how are we to classify a puppet with an operative mouth, and operative eyes and eyebrows as well, but with no other movement, such as most ventriloquists' dummies? Remarkably enough, such dummies are scarcely mentioned in the literature of puppetry, although they are one of puppetry's most popular manifestations in the West.

It seems absurd to call any of these puppets rod-puppets, since, excepting Kermit, they have no rods whatsoever; but they fit no better anywhere else in the object-control taxonomy. At least one new classification seems required: mouth-moving puppets. And given the particular qualities of the ventriloquist's dummy, a second new classification seems required as well.

Beaumont next lists jigging-puppets, and at last we find brief respite from controversy. McPharlin also lists this type, but it is ignored by Blackham and Arnott, as by many others. McPharlin writes of jigging-puppets:

> They are the types one sees as toys on city street-corners before Christmas, a pair of feathered dancers which hop with uncanny life, midway along a string one end of which is tied to a post, the other to the animator's knee; or the jigging darkies [sic] whose feet are set into flight by the vibrations of a board, pounded at its attached end by the fist of the operator. The movement range of such puppets is too restricted and little controllable for artistic use. (1938: 88–89)

The latter of the two examples given by McPharlin is also known as a marionette à la planchette (Beaumont 1958: 18).

McPharlin's dismissal of the artistic value of the jigging-puppet is harsh but appropriate: these puppets can, indeed, do little but jig. One may wonder whether they are not merely toys, rather than theatrical figures at all. No doubt they are most often used as toys; but given the context of street-corner performance as described by McPharlin, they must, according to all of the definitions discussed in Part I, be considered puppets.

The jigging-puppet exemplifies yet another problem with the object-control method: such a minor type of puppet scarcely seems to merit taxonomic ranking with widespread and highly developed types such as the shadow-puppet and the marionette. But because it is unique in being controlled by semirandom vibration, and because it has a long, if not illustrious, history in the West, the object-control method usually gives it desultory mention.

Following on Beaumont's list come "glove-puppets, or hand-puppets," and once more we must enter the fray. The distinguishing features of the hand-puppet are universally agreed upon. Arnott explains that "the figures have a hollow head and arms and a long, sleeve-like body; the operator inserts his hand in the body and controls head and arms with his fingers" (1964: 58). "Punch and Judy" is the archetypical example of hand-puppetry, and the hand-puppet appears on every list.

And yet, in an essay on the history of puppetry, Jurkowski comments that "the glove puppet and the shadow puppet . . . stand outside the art of puppetry" (1967 [1965]: 26). He does not articulate his objection to the shadow-puppet, but elsewhere he paraphrases the early twentieth-century German scholar Fritz Eichler to the effect that "the glove puppet is not to be considered as 'pure' puppet, for it is actually the hand of the puppet-player which is its soul. The glove puppet is thus a 'prolongation' of the actor . . . [and should be considered] as an extension of mime theatre" (1988 [1979]: 21–22).

Eichler's argument, as stated by Jurkowski, is predicated on the idea that the operator's living hand inside the figure is the real focus of the audience's attention, and that what is perceived as the hand-puppet is no more than a costume for that hand; the figure is not "separated from the body of its manipulator," and does not follow "its own mechanical laws" (1988 [1979]: 22). Thus, Punch is not actually a puppet at all; neither, for that matter, is Kermit, who also is scarcely more than the costumed hand of its operator. How is one to resolve whether the hand-puppet, and all puppets that are based upon the operator's hand, are or are not puppets?

One might begin by admitting that the human hand is, metaphorically, the "soul" of the hand-puppet, but that the hand-puppet remains something other than the human hand. As we have seen, Obraztsov suggests that this otherness arises from the perception of the audience that the living hand is "apart" from its operator, "with a rhythm and a character of its own" (1950: 155). Or, as we have argued, the audience perceives the figure presented by the hand as if it were an object, in the same manner as it would perceive any object. In mime theatre, the audience perceives the mime as a whole living human figure; in hand-puppetry, the audience perceives the operating hand as divorced from the human operator, and as an object in its own right. This perception of the hand, whether costumed or bare, distinguishes it from mime.

One might continue by noting that Jurkowski himself comments that, "for the public, [hand-puppets] are puppets because they are artificial creatures, they behave in their own typical way, and they are able to present different characters on the stage" (1988 [1983]: 76–77). This comment exposes an important point: the dismissal of the hand-puppet is based on an a priori assumption that the puppet must be a wholly inanimate object operated in some mechanical way; but what is the basis for this assumption? The popular standard relies only on the audience's perception of the puppet as an "artificial creature"; what matters for this standard, quite properly, is that the puppet is perceived as if it were an object.

One might conclude by noting that Jurkowski speaks of the hand-puppet as being able "to present different characters on the stage." This ability of the puppet, to present a character that the audience might imagine to have a spurious life of its own, inescapably separates it from mime theatre. The puppet can be imagined to have life owing to the deployed signs of design, movement, and speech that are its entire existence; the mime, in contrast, is actually alive, and whatever performance signs he or she might employ, that life is never in question. The object-control method, because it classifies puppets according to their nature as objects and their manner of control, makes objections to the hand-puppet possible. But contrary to the object-control method, neither the nature of the object nor the manner of control has any bearing on whether a particular theatrical figure is a puppet.

This whole matter also reintroduces the problem of distinguishing the puppet from the live actor in a mask or costume. Consider the Muppets' Big Bird, in which the operator is entirely inside the theatrical figure, giving direct motivation to the figure in its entirety (Henson Associates 1980: 9,16). Following Eichler, if not Jurkowski, Big Bird would have to be seen as an "extension of mime theatre." But following our earlier analysis, it would be recognized as a puppet, because its physiognomy is distinct from that of its operator, while the Mickey Mouse previously discussed is far more clearly the costume and mask of a living actor. How then should Big Bird be classified? The object-control method gives not a hint.

We must also wonder, as we did in our discussion of rod-puppets, at the range of figures to be classified as hand-puppets. We have seen how the Muppet-style puppet defies being typed as a rod-puppet; no less does it defy classification as a hand-puppet. Despite being based on its operator's hand, it is quite distinct from the traditional hand-puppet, most obviously in its operative mouth. The object-control taxonomy simply cannot account for it.

And then there is the traditional Korean puppet. In a survey of Korean theatre history, Oh-Kon Cho writes:

> The Korean puppet . . . does not belong to any of the most familiar puppet categories. . . . Instead, it combines aspects of [many types]. The body of the Korean puppet, the main stick, is held by the hand, which is reminiscent of the hand puppet; its arms, somewhat like the marionette, are manipulated by strings, from below; and the unique quality of arm movement reminds some audiences of the characteristic stiff mobilization of the rod puppet. (1988: 309)

Such a puppet seems specifically designed to torment object-control taxonomists, and presents yet another difficulty with objections to the hand-puppet. The Korean puppet is constructed in a manner similar to that of the traditional hand-puppet, but instead of the operator's fingers having direct control of the head and arms, the head is controlled via a central rod, while the arms are controlled by strings (Cho 1979: 27). To an audience unfamiliar with its construction and operation, it might, at first glance, appear to be a traditional hand-puppet; its movement would also appear to be like a hand-puppet's, differing only in that it would not be as capable at bending at the neck and waist, and in that its arms would tend to move up and down, like a rod-puppet's, rather than in and out.

In fact, a number of Western puppet companies make a practice of taking traditional hand-puppets and running a central rod through the costume, into the head, while still operating the puppet's hands from inside the costume with their fingers. The advantage of this technique is that it takes the weight of the puppet's head off of the operator's "head" finger, making it easier for the operator to keep the puppet in action for an extended period of time.

In both of these cases, the puppet retains its hand-puppet appearance and much of its hand-puppet movement, but loses what Eichler calls its "soul." If the living hand is so easily, even casually, dismissed, how much should we care about the soul of the puppet, as long as the puppet is perceived as an object and imagined to have life?

Returning to our discussion of the classification of the hand-puppet, we must next consider how the object-control method might classify a puppet that certainly involves the hand, but can scarcely be said to be a true object in need of control.

This problem is presented not only by puppetry such as Burr Tillstrom's bare-handed sketch about the Berlin Wall, or by the renowned French performer Yves Joly's performances with gloved hands (see Obraztsov 1985 [1981]: 265–69); the pervasive, if undocumented, use of living hands in conjunction with a light source to create shadows on a screen or a wall has no place in the object-control taxonomy. Neither has the equally pervasive and undocumented use of bare living fists, clenched so that the pivoting of the thumb represents the movement of a mouth. It would seem absurd to classify these as hand-puppets, given the universally accepted description of the hand-puppet, but what else could they be called? The object-control method can neither classify nor name such puppetry, although that is what it is, if only of a rudimentary kind.

Next on Beaumont's list we find "magnetically controlled puppets." This is the most idiosyncratic of Beaumont's classifications, and it does not appear on any of our other lists. Beaumont himself mentions only one example, in the work of a Mr. Cecil Brinton, before giving up on the subject (1958: 18).

The distinguishing characteristic of the magnetically controlled puppet seems not to be the magnetism itself, but the fact that control is effected without physical contact between the controlling mechanism and the puppet. If Beaumont were writing today, he would probably broaden this classification to include electronically controlled puppets, or, audio-animatronic puppets, which are similarly motivated, at least in part, without direct contact between the electronic mechanism of control and the electronic mechanism inside the puppet (Henson Associates 1980: 13).

Discussion of puppets that are controlled, via magnetism or electronics, without physical contact, reintroduces the problem of distinguishing the puppet from the automaton. The rather sedate figures that wave to pleasure-seekers on the rides at Disneyland, and the notoriously loud figures that assault the sensibilities of adults who take their children to Chuck E. Cheese pizzerias, seem to be automata rather than animatronic puppets. But what is the basis for this distinction?

No inherent distinction can be drawn in terms of their design: the Chuck E. Cheese musical ensemble looks more or less like the Electric Mayhem, the Muppets' musical band. Neither is there an inherent distinction in terms of speech: music is directly attributed to both groups, and in both cases, the music is prerecorded. There is, however, an inherent distinction in their movement, or, more precisely, in their movement possibilities: the Chuck E. Cheese ensemble can move only in the manner and sequence for which they have been programmed; the Muppet musicians are responsive to the control of their operators, and their movement can never be predicted in regard to manner or sequence.

It should be noted that this comparison is somewhat misleading, in that the Muppet band is not, in fact, electronically controlled. But even if it were, and even if this control limited the manner of their movement, the sequence of their movements would still be at the discretion of their operators.

The distinction, then, between the automaton and the puppet is one of potential for movement. Although a brief viewing of the two might lead the audience to believe that they are functionally interchangeable, prolonged viewing would expose the fact that the automaton cannot sustain the audience's imagination of life, owing to its relative poverty of movement possibilities, while the puppet can.

To return to Beaumont: the listing of the magnetically controlled puppet exposes a fundamental weakness of the object-control method that we have noted before; there is an infinite number of possible objects that may be used as puppets, and an as yet unknown number of means of control. The object-control taxonomy has no way of allowing for new objects, new means of control, or new combinations of object and control. The best it can do is simply to add each new type to the list, whenever the work of a "Mr. Cecil Brinton" is noticed, as Beaumont has added the magnetically controlled puppet. But such a list, endlessly added onto, is worse than cumbersome: it fails, ultimately, to allow for meaningful comparison and contrast of puppets.

Beaumont's final listing is of "Japanese three-man puppets," or, as they are more commonly known, Bunraku puppets. Arnott leaves them off his list entirely, although he is aware of their existence (1964: 79–80); perhaps he realizes the futility of fitting them into a system of description dominated by Western concepts. As we have already discussed our Japanese performance example at some length, we need only note here that the object-control method classifies Bunraku as sui generis, essentially giving up the synchronic approach and adopting the taxonomic principles of the historic-geographic method.

Thus is exhausted, in more ways than one, Beaumont's list of types. As we have seen, it groups together puppets that are quite dissimilar, and ignores many other puppets entirely. Indeed, if one were of a mind to work within its limitations, one could probably work out a more coherent and comprehensive set of classifications; but its limitations would seem to render the exercise moot.

The theory imbedded in the object-control method is, as will be obvious by now, that puppets are inanimate objects of a limited number of distinct and established types, and that the manner of control is their most important element. As should also be obvious by now, this theory is untenable. Puppets may or may not be inanimate objects, the number of their types is unlimited, and the manner of their control describes surprisingly little about them.

Beyond matters of object and control, the method offers little descriptive vocabulary. There is but limited discussion of the design and movement possibilities available to the puppet, and no discussion at all of the speech possibilities, since object and control have no bearing upon them. It seems astonishing that a theory of puppetry would be willing to forego detailed discussion of design and movement, and to forego any discussion of speech, but such is the case with the object-control method. It fails to acknowledge that puppets exist to perform, and thus avoids discussing the complexities of puppet performance.

To conclude: the historic-geographic and object-control taxonomies do not allow for a full description of the puppet. The historic-geographic taxonomy, using a diachronic method, relies on arbitrary temporal and geographic distinctions to avoid being overwhelmed by the sheer variety of puppet traditions. The method might be justified if it were actually to consider each of the distinct traditions and discover how they have developed and influenced one another over time and across space, but the relative paucity of information on many puppet traditions, and the lack of an adequate vocabulary for description of those traditions for which we do have information, have thus far made it impossible to use the method to much purpose.

The object-control taxonomy, an attempt at synchronic analysis, postulates up to seven types of puppet control, but the distinctions drawn between these types are quite vague, and the types themselves fail to accommodate a number of distinct control methods. Owing to its concentration on the manner of control, the method offers limited information about the design and movement, and no information at all about the speech, of the puppet.

If, as has been argued above, the puppet is perceived as an object, yet imagined to have life, owing to its deployment of abstracted signs of life in the three sign-systems of design, movement, and speech, then it follows that description of the puppet must include systematic information concerning all of its sign-systems. It would be foolish, of course, to abandon the descriptive vocabularies of the two standard taxonomies, for traditions based on the particulars of history and geography obviously exist, and the manner of puppet control is obviously important. But these vocabularies must be substantially augmented, and set within the context of a more encompassing theory, if we are to hope for a full description of the puppet.

5

A NEW BASIS FOR
DESCRIPTION

It is beyond the scope of this study to attempt a complete diachronic taxonomy of the puppet, which would be tantamount to outlining the global history of puppetry. As has already been explained, too little information as yet exists on which to base such an outline, and too sparse a vocabulary is available for the explication of such an outline. Nothing can be done here to alleviate the lack of information; but we can certainly aid in the development of the necessary vocabulary by examining how the puppet, as a distinctive theatrical phenomenon, can be made to deploy signs from each of the three sign-systems that allow it to fulfill the audience's psychological desire to imagine it as having life. We will examine each of the sign-systems in turn, and consider the variables within each sign-system, the location of particular signs deployed or generated through these variables along the puppet's continuum of representation, and the relationships between the three sign-systems themselves.

Before delving into the sign-systems, however, it will be useful to consider the general nature of the puppet's signs. Edward Gordon Craig, indicting naturalism in the live theatre, cries out: "Do away with the real tree, do away with the reality of delivery, do away with the reality of action, and you tend towards doing away with the actor. . . . No longer would there be a living figure to confuse us into connecting actuality and art" (1911: 81). Of course, it might be argued that "actuality and art" are not necessarily antithetical, but Craig's indictment makes an essential point. There is nothing of actuality, or, one might say, of real life, in the puppet; there is only art, the signs themselves that constitute the puppet.

We have seen that the puppet's abstracted signs can be located along a continuum of representation that ranges from the imitative to the stylized to the conceptual, according to the quality and quantity of the signs. Almost every writer on puppetry recognizes the importance of sign quality and quantity: "A puppet must always be more than his live counterpart — simpler, sadder, more wicked, more supple. The puppet is an essence and an emphasis" (Baird 1965: 15); "[Puppets] must condense, synthesize, all that is essential and characteristic in the various features of human nature" (Obraztsov 1967 [1965]: 20); innumerable such citations could be adduced.

Proschan highlights the puppet's limited sign quantity by means of a useful analogy:

> Just as a word is abbreviated by the removal of certain letters and the preservation of only the most important, so theatrical signs utilize only the most crucial markers of their referents. However, unlike words, abbreviation of theatrical signs does not necessarily result in a reduction in size or mass, just a reduction in the density or quantity of elements. (1983: 38n)

The puppet, however, does more than just reduce sign quantity, for the "most crucial markers" that are preserved are themselves changed in quality, owing to the limitation of their number itself, and to the exaggerations to which they are then subjected.

Green and Pepicello offer an insight into the particularly theatrical nature of the puppet's signs:

> When puppets "speak," they [might] move their jaws, and usually gesture, but these behaviors are not the source of the sound. . . . Thus, although we have a part of the human speech-making process manifested by the puppet, it constitutes no more than a sign for speech production. . . . Similarly, puppets do not actually walk; they are moved by the puppeteer. Movement from one area of the stage to another could

be managed far more easily and efficiently than by making a marionette imitate human locomotion. Therefore, no simple logistics are at work here. . . . The marionette displays a mere sign of animation. (1983: 153)

This analysis might seem obvious, but, in fact, it contains an important insight: the signs deployed by the puppet are as intentional as theatrical signs can be; their intent, whether or not this is acknowledged by the puppet-artist, is to lead the audience to imagine life while it perceives an object. Indeed, "no simple logistics are at work here"; the puppet's abstracted signs of life provoke the process of double-vision.

But while the puppet is very much intentional, can it be said to be fully intentional? Elam notes that in the live theatre, "the audience starts with the assumption that every detail is an intentional sign and whatever cannot be related to the representation as such is converted into a sign of the actor's very reality—it is not, in any case, excluded from semiosis" (1980: 9). In puppetry, however, there is no living actor toward whose reality signs unrelated to the representation may be converted. Or, to turn the matter around, there is no living actor to deploy random and unintentional signs. And so Veltruský suggests: "A puppet which represents a character has only those features of a real person which are needed for the given dramatic situation; all of the components of the puppet are intentional signs" (quoted in Proschan 1983: 15).

This is generally the puppet-artist's desire, but Veltruský overstates the case. Unintentional signs will inevitably be intermixed with intended ones. The execution of the puppet's design will never completely overcome the intractability of the material out of which it is wrought; the manipulation that creates movement will never completely overcome the mechanical quirks of the puppet in operation and the physical limitations of the puppet-operator(s); and the vocal performance will be subject to the vocal limitations of the puppet-speaker(s).

And it is worse than that. Even if the puppet's signs were to be deployed exactly as intended, and without any unintentional signs intermixed, the audience might acknowledge these signs in unintended ways. Signs invariably convey a multiplicity of meanings beyond the control of the artist, and no artist can fully fathom the breadth of meanings that might be inferred by the audience in response to any given sign. What's more, as we have seen Proschan suggest, the audience must not only acknowledge the deployed signs, but also fill in the blanks between the signs; that is, it must add those signs that have been left out of the abbreviation. Although the artist might direct this activity of filling in, he or she cannot control it. The puppet is surely as intentional a performer as the theatre can provide. But it is not, and cannot be, fully intentional. If such a limitation keeps puppetry from attaining the status of precise science, this is only to be expected, for puppetry is an art, and all art conveys meanings both intentional and unintentional.

Filling in the blanks is an important part of puppet performance. The puppet's signs are never a complete set of signs of life, no matter how the puppet might be made to imitate life. The audience is required to add, in some way, to the deployed signs, so that they might imagine the object to have life. Of course, the audience has its psychological desire to fill in the blanks, to accord the puppet its "life." Perhaps one reason for the intensity of audience involvement in puppet theatre arises from the audience's role as co-creator of the performance. This role involves the co-creation of comedy through verbal interplay, as Proschan discusses (1987: 30–44), but extends beyond it to include the co-creation of implied signs, and even, as we have seen, of "consciousness," for the puppet.

According to Iván Koós, a director and designer for the Budapest State Puppet Theatre:

> The most important thing in the visual representation of the puppet stage is that it sets something going in the spectator's imagination without finishing the process. At a certain point the idea is left open to be completed by the spectator. . . . Take a familiar example: some of the puppets have no mouths, yet the spectator has the feeling that at certain appropriate moments the puppet smiles or gives expression to its sentiments by facial mimicry. (quoted in Gál 1978: 20)

This principle is operative in all three of the puppet's sign-systems; it is a vital, if often unrecognized, aspect of all puppet performance.

The realization that the puppet is constituted of signs from three particular sign-systems was made, as we have seen in the introduction, centuries ago by the court poet to the Javanese King Airlangga. It has been taken up with great vigor, not surprisingly, by scholars from the field of semiotics. It will be recalled that in Jurkowski's definition of the puppet theatre, the puppet is referred to as a "speaking and performing [that is, moving] object" (1988 [1983]: 79). Veltruský also discusses the three sign-systems, and suggests that the puppet's signs "convey meaning by similarity":

> The inanimate object is more or less similar to a human or anthropomorphic being. The physical action imposed on it is more or less similar to the actions and behavior of the same represented being. . . . The voice performance also signifies the voice performance of the represented being by similarity . . . [although it differs from the others in being real in itself, so that] the *signans* and the *signatum* are here existentially the same; some voice modifiers used in puppetry tend to attenuate or suppress this feature. (1983: 71)

The "more or less similar" relation of the puppet to life is what we have called the varying quality and quantity of the puppet's abstracted signs. Veltruský's characterization of the puppet as an "inanimate object" is, as we have seen, unfortunate, and in need of modification. In using the terms *signans* and *signatum,* he means that the sign-system of speech differs from the other sign-systems in that signs of live speech are conveyed by live speech itself, whether or not they are attributed to the puppet.

Green and Pepicello agree that the sign-system of speech is different. They write that "*channels* . . . are systems consisting of a message source, a medium of transmission (for our purposes, either visual or auditory), and a receiver" (1983: 147). They then note that, in the visual channel, "a scaled-down system of kinesics . . . creates a conventional code by focusing on a selected set of movements by the puppet figure," and also that "a second code functioning in the visual channel is the physical appearance of the puppet itself" (1983: 151); that is, they note what this study has called the sign-systems of movement and design. Within the auditory channel they note "a simplified or scaled-down system of speech" (1983: 148). For Green and Pepicello, the sign-system of speech differs from the others in that it makes use of a separate channel of transmission.

The differences between, and the relative importance of, the sign-systems of movement and speech are matters of substantial dispute. As we have seen, many artists, such as McPharlin, Obraztsov, and Baird, follow Duranty in asserting that "what the puppets do entirely dominates what they say" (quoted in Veltruský 1983: 97), while many scholars, such as Jurkowski and Veltruský, follow Magnin in asserting that "the separation of word and action is precisely that which constitutes the puppet play" (quoted in Proschan 1983: 20). The differences between, and the relative importance of, these sign-systems will be taken up later in this chapter.

Following is a chart that correlates three basic points on the continuum of sign representation with the three sign-systems of the puppet; beneath each of the sign-systems are listed the major variables that allow for the variation of quality and quantity of the representative signs. All of the terms used in this chart will be explained in our examination of the sign-systems themselves.

	Design	**Movement**	**Speech**
Imitative	Lifelike	With the Puppet	Character
Stylized	Selection/ Exaggeration	Despite the Puppet	Caricature
Conceptual	Unlifelike/ Operator Present	Against the Puppet	Voice Modified/ Speaker Present
Variables	Features	Control Mechanics	Paralinguistics
	Size	Control Points	Dialect/Language
	Materials	Articulation Points	Voice Modification
	Operator Presence	Lighting/Scenery	Speaker Presence

The three charted points on the continuum of sign representation are nothing more than its end points and a point at its middle. Given the nearly infinite number of possible permutations of the variables within each sign-system, and given the synergistic nature of these permutations, it will be impossible to locate with total accuracy the place of each sign along the continuum. But the chart will help us ascribe general location to the signs, and understand the manner in which such ascription can be made.

It should be noted that there seems to be no precedent for such a charting out of the puppet's sign-systems; thus, at present, our effort can be considered nothing more than a tentative effort to organize discussion of puppet signs.

It should also be noted that diachronic questions will inevitably seep into this discussion of signs. For example, does the on-stage presence of puppet-operators in Bunraku have a different significance for Japanese and non-Japanese audiences? Or, to put the question another way: does the existence of certain performance conventions entail differing acknowledgments of the puppet by differing audiences? There can be no doubt that localized performance conventions are an important aspect of puppetry, and this would need to be addressed in any diachronic account. One of the purposes of the synchronic account that follows is to develop a means for identifying such conventions for diachronic discussion. For this study, it is a sufficient task to identify and discuss the range of possibilities in puppet signification.

THE SIGN-SYSTEM OF DESIGN

The signs of design for a puppet are, or can be, intentionally deployed to a degree that cannot be matched by live theatre. As we have seen, the signs may be entirely inanimate in nature, a mixture of animate and inanimate, or entirely animate. Batchelder writes:

[The artist] can give [the puppet] whatever grace or dignity or distortion or ugliness the play demands. He selects those physical characteristics which are essential to a given character, and expresses them with simplicity and force. He is not hampered . . . by the limitations of human anatomy. Furthermore, he is not confined to the representation of human beings. (1947: 281)

Our concern here is not to discuss all of the choices puppet-artists can make in designing puppets; rather, it is to set out the most important variables of puppet design, and to describe how they are used to create abstracted signs of life. These variables include the features and size of the puppet, the physical material that it presents to the audience, and the on-stage absence or presence of its operator(s).

The features of the puppet are anatomical details, such as eyes, nose, mouth, and limbs, as well as the general shape of the puppet. Many traditions dictate the quantity and quality of the puppet's feature-signs. In our Japanese example, "there are roughly forty different types of heads in general use . . . and about thirty special ones"; the differences between these types depend upon the characteristics of the features, "male and female, young, old and middle-aged, good and evil—each with its own refinements" (Adachi 1985: 87). All such features, however, are to a great extent equally representational in quality and quantity. That is, all of the puppet heads have features of a nearly lifelike quality, and all of them have a full complement of such features, including ears, although these are often covered by wigs. Additionally, all of the puppets have arms that are lifelike in design; male puppets have lifelike legs as well, while female puppets have costumes that hide the absence of legs.

In our Javanese example there is also traditional dictation of the quality and quantity of feature-signs:

> The several hundred human, god, and ogre figures . . . can be classified and identified through some twenty-five physical features. Body build, foot stance, nose shape, eye shape, and the slant of the head are five of the most crucial. According to the most detailed Javanese texts, there are thirteen different eye shapes, thirteen nose shapes, and two or three types each of body build, foot stance, and slant of head. These different types of features can be combined into dozens of identifiable puppet types. (Brandon 1970: 40–41)

Again, the features of various puppets are, to a great extent, equally representational in quality and quantity. The facial features are very much stylized in quality, with the shapes of the eyes, noses, and mouths being substantially exaggerated. The shapes of the bodies and the arms are also exaggerated, to an almost grotesque degree: the bodies tend to be either emaciated or swollen, while the arms, fully extended, might exceed the height of the full figure (Malkin 1977: 108–109). The quantity of features for these shadow-puppets is substantial, including the full gamut of facial features and limbs. It is subjected to a certain amount of selection, however, in that most of the puppets are presented in profile: while all four limbs are always visible, only half of a "full" face can be seen at any given time.

The Japanese Bunraku feature-signs are of a near lifelike quality and quantity, whereas the Javanese shadow-puppet feature-signs are of a stylized quality and quantity; both are dictated by tradition. But of course, such signs need not be so dictated, and may be freely chosen for deployment. A description of some puppets from the Budapest State Puppet Theatre's production of *The Miraculous Mandarin* demonstrates the manner in which puppets having different quality and quantity of feature-signs can be used together:

> The ruffians have no faces. Their convex chests bulge like the abdomens of huge insects. The girl's face is also empty: her puppet-like appearance is emphasized by the absence of eyes, nose, or mouth; nothing but a blank oval is there. Her character can be seen in her seductively twisting limbs, slim long legs and inviting arms. When the Mandarin appears he looks the most human of all the figures, magically strange as he is. The Mandarin has a face. He has human features. Among the faceless, pounded into a shapeless mass, he represents humanity. (Gál 1978: 28)

In this production, the ruffians and the girl have highly stylized features: the exaggerated quality of their body-shapes denotes their nature; this quality is enhanced by the absence, the total lack of quantity, of facial features. The Mandarin, by pointed contrast, is nearly lifelike in his features' quality and quantity. The effect of such a contrast should not be underestimated. Through the deployment of varying feature-signs, the characters are profoundly distinguished.

There does not seem to be any major Eurasian tradition that regularly relies on unlifelike feature-signs for the puppet itself. Malkin has told us, however, that "African puppets often bear little resemblance to Western concepts of how puppets should look" (1977: 71); this suggests that unlifelike feature-signs might not be uncommon in African traditions. And of course, they are quite common in many contemporary productions.

Turning to another production of the Budapest State Puppet Theatre, we learn that "the characters in *Aventures* are [represented by] objects. They are: a suit on a hanger, an umbrella, a uniform cap, a lady's wig and hat, stoles, fur necklets . . . and so on. From these objects the human tragicomedy, the philosophical play evolves" (Gál 1978: 40). The feature-signs of the represented characters, a man and a woman, are subjected to a radical process of selection: all that remains are what seem to be elements of their costumes and props. Nonetheless, these elements combine, with the vital assistance of movement and speech, to create characters. The feature-signs of these puppets are so unlifelike as to render the puppets unrecognizable, outside of the performance, as puppets at all.

While the feature-signs of the characters in *Aventures* are subjected to a radical selection, those signs that survive do not undergo an equally radical exaggeration: the suit, the wig, and so on, are clearly what they are. The process of metonymy, the representation of something by one or more of its attributes, is certainly, although not exclusively, involved in such representation.

Feature-signs, however, can also be made unlifelike through radical exaggeration, in which a metaphoric process takes the place of the metonymic one. Bil Baird has, in a science-fiction sketch, a puppet character named "Crutchface." It is constructed of four pieces of wood: one is shaped like a swollen banana, with the gash of a mouth above its lower end; another is a small cylinder, with the dark irises of eyes on its ends, which penetrates the first just above mid-height and juts out on both sides; two more are shaped like tuning forks, whose one-legged ends touch the ground, and in whose forked ends the ends of the "eye" cylinder rest, suggesting these tuning fork pieces to be legs (1965: 219).

Quantitative selection of feature-signs is present here, in that Crutchface has no torso or arms. But more important is the qualitative exaggeration and juxtaposition of those features that remain: the shapes of the head and eyes are exaggerated beyond the grotesque, and are scarcely more than concepts; the attachment of the legs to the eyes is shocking, and suggestive of an utterly deformed personality. Crutch-face is perhaps too crude a name for a puppet whose feature-signs are deployed, through radical exaggeration, with such metaphoric force.

The feature-signs in the design of the puppet, then, range from the imitative to the stylized to the conceptual, according to whether they are lifelike in quality and quantity, whether their quantity has been sub-jected to some selection, and their quality to some exaggeration, or whether their quality and/or quantity have been so radically altered as to render them unlifelike.

The next variable of design to consider is that of the puppet's size. McPharlin contends that "the only time when puppet size is of conse-quence is when [the puppet is] purposely contrasted with the human scale" (1938: 75). Although such a contrast with the human scale cer-tainly has significant consequences, McPharlin is wrong in contending that the sign of the puppet's size is otherwise inconsequential.

An understanding of the consequences of size requires recognition that size-signs work in two distinct ways. The first is when the puppet is contrasted with its stage, with its scenery and/or props, and/or with other puppets with which it appears; this may be called the relative size of the puppet. The audience perceives the puppet not according to any human notion of scale, but in a relative sense, according to the scale established in the presentation itself. The second way is when the pup-pet is contrasted, purposely or not, with the human scale; this may be called the absolute size of the puppet. The audience perceives the pup-pet, in an absolute sense, to be larger than life-size, or near life-size, or smaller than life-size.

The relative size of the puppet generates meaning by its contrast to other puppets or to its surroundings. This sign is not, as we have seen with McPharlin, generally recognized by writers on puppetry. Batchelder remarks:

People unfamiliar with puppets are often surprised to find that the fig-ures which seemed life size when on the stage, are actually quite small. . . . Basically, it is simply a matter of the relationship between the pup-

pet and its surroundings; furniture, scenery, and properties are designed
in proportion to the figures, and the eye accepts the whole scene as life
size unless something in the human scale is suddenly introduced into the
composition. (1947: 284)

Batchelder refers here to a conventional puppet theatre illusion, in
which everything on the puppet-stage, including the stage itself, is uni-
formly scaled down in size. But like McPharlin, she seems oblivious to
the possibility of deploying large puppets along with small ones, or of
deploying puppets of any size amid surroundings of a differing scale.

In our Javanese example, the puppets differ substantially in size from
one another. This relative discrepancy is not a function of naturalistic
height differences; that is, it is not a matter of small babies and large
adults. H. Ulbricht, a contemporary German scholar, points out that,
generally, "the bigger they are, the more violent is their nature. Spiritual characters are slim and small in size" (1970: 7).

Similarly, relative size-signs are deployed in the Liège puppet tradition. In this case, however, relative size is employed with a reversed
conventional hierarchy:

> Large figures [are] stronger or more noble than small figures. In this
> way, Charlemagne might be nearly five feet tall, while a minor charac-
> ter might be less than eighteen inches high. (Malkin 1977: 24–25)

The relative size of the puppets in both these traditions is an intentional
violation of the conventional illusion of puppet size as referred to by
McPharlin and Batchelder, and is anything but inconsequential, as it
conveys, through conventional understanding, vital information about
the characters being represented.

Signs of relative size may also be used to establish the puppet's relationship with its surroundings. Obraztsov details such usage in a production by the Moscow State Central Puppet Theatre:

> We wanted to show a Ukrainian village at the moment when the
> church service is at an end and the villagers are making for their homes.
> Our stage in this scene consisted of five gradually ascending horizontal
> planes. In the foreground stood large huts, immediately behind were
> smaller ones, and in the extreme background was a small church.

For each [of the characters] we made five different sizes of puppets, varying in height from four inches to two foot six. Small puppets emerged from the church, went off in all directions and disappeared behind the huts and trees. From behind the trees bigger puppets emerged on to the next plane, then even bigger ones, and when they appeared right in the foreground they were quite large. In this way we achieved perspective. (1954: 13–14)

The Pickwick Puppet Theatre similarly used relative size in its 1980 production of *Don Quixote*, directed by Ken Moses. Puppets of the hero and of Sancho Panza ranged from eight inches to eight feet in height, and were variously used to create what amounted to cinematic-style long-shots and close-ups, the smallest puppets being almost lost in the vast landscape of the stage, the largest ones dominating the stage with their overwhelming presence.

The absolute size of the puppet is a sign that conveys meaning not by contrast to its surroundings or to other puppets, but intrinsically. The hand-puppet, with its diminutive stature, can scarcely help but seem charming and playful. We have seen that the metaphorical associations arising from its toylike size can have a substantial impact on its audience. We have also seen, in our English consideration, how the hand-puppet Punch is allowed great license to say and do things that would be insupportable in the live theatre, and might be equally insupportable if said or done by puppets of greatly larger size. It may well be that Punch is protected not only by his general status as a puppet, but by his particular status as a hand-puppet — that is, by the charm and playfulness associated with his absolute size.

Conversely, the greater-than-life-size puppet, with its overwhelming stature, can scarcely help but seem powerful and foreboding. We have seen that the metaphorical associations arising from its godlike size can have their own substantial impact on its audience. In our American example, *The Enchanted Child*, only two characters are represented by greater-than-life-size puppets: the child's mother and his schoolteacher, both of whom can lead the child into paroxysms of dread. The Bread and Puppet Theatre uses towering puppets that extend up to twelve feet in height. These puppets have "power, stature, and dignity, and [they] . . . predispose [the company] to the presentation of a somber view of human existence" (Brecht 1988 1: 304). It may well be that they predispose a "somber view of life" precisely because of the hint of awesome deity associated with their absolute size.

The size-signs in the design of the puppet are not as easy to categorize along the continuum of representation as are the feature-signs. Although there are more ways in which they may be deployed than is generally recognized, the choices they offer are not nearly as extensive as those of feature-signs. This is because size-signs can be altered only in quality; for any given puppet, there can be no reduction in their quantity, since each puppet has only one size, however many puppets are used to represent a particular character. One may suggest, however, that when size-signs are deployed to create the conventional illusion of the puppet theatre as referred to by McPharlin and Batchelder, their quality is lifelike and imitative; when they are relative, and emphasize relations between puppets or with surroundings, their quality has been subjected to exaggeration and they are stylized; and when they are absolute, and extreme enough to convey meaning by their extremity, their quality is unlifelike and conceptual.

The next variable to consider in the sign-system of design is that of the materials that the puppet presents to the audience. Batchelder comments: "Puppets being imaginative creatures, freedom can be taken with the materials out of which they are constructed" (1947: 284). This freedom finds expression in three different ways: materials may be chosen because they are inexpensive, because they are easy to work, or because they have communicative meanings of their own. The first two reasons do not concern us here; our concern is with the communicative meaning of material-signs.

McPharlin cites a list of puppet materials offered by E. Gordon Craig—"paper, cardboard, hide, zinc, wood, cloth, papier mâché, and gesso"—to which he adds "various modern synthetics, such as Plastic Wood; rubber, cut or molded; ceramics . . . [as well as] other special materials, [such as] metal, glass, stone, [and] fiber" (1938: 71–72). To this already extensive list may be added virtually any material known to humanity, including, as we have seen, the living flesh of the puppet-operator.

McPharlin goes on to assert that "materials may be used for their own visual and tactile qualities [for example] glass, copper, and feathers for transparency, malleability, and lightness, either for fittingness to the design or for symbolic quality" (1938: 73). This assertion is confirmed by Péter Molnár Gál, a designer for the Budapest State Puppet Theatre: "The material chosen . . . may in itself have something to convey. It can affect the spectator on its own account and evoke associations and feelings in art-lovers" (1978: 17).

It will be recalled that the Budapest State Puppet Theatre's production of *The Miraculous Mandarin* had ruffians whose faces were made of featureless leather. The use of leather for these faces is as significant as their lack of features, for leather provokes associations of callousness. If the faces were of a featureless white gauze, the associations would be entirely different. The material-sign of leather is vital to the design, and to the characterization, of the puppets.

The exercise of imagining familiar puppets with altered material-signs demonstrates the importance of such signs. One of the many reasons for the success of the Muppets, for example, would seem to be that their supple faces are not only capable of expressive motion, but are also rather comforting in their very softness. If characters such as, say, Bert and Ernie were made with precisely the same features, but of a lustrous metal, or of leather, or even of wood, the effect of the material-signs would be substantially altered.

The material-signs of the puppet can, but need not always, include the costume of the puppet. Adachi quotes a Japanese costume-maker: "In Bunraku, the puppet is the costume, the costume is the character" (1985: 119). This overstates the case, for, as we have seen, there are forty different types of heads for Bunraku puppets, carefully distinguished by their features. If the costume were, indeed, the character, there would be no need for such elaboration of the puppets' heads. Costumes are, however, a fundamental part of most puppets' design, and the foregoing discussion of material-signs must be taken to include the materials of the puppet's costume.

The material-signs in the design of the puppet are no easier to categorize along the continuum of representation than are size-signs. Each of the materials we have mentioned, and all of those that have gone unmentioned, such as buttons used for eyes, zippers for mouths, fabrics, bristles or wigs for hair, and so on, has its own particular quality. While every puppet deploys at least one material-sign, most puppets deploy more than one; when consideration is given also to the puppet's costume, the quantity of material-signs deployed by any particular puppet can quickly become quite numerous indeed.

It would seem safe to suggest, however, that when material-signs are deployed in a relatively self-effacing way, as is often the case with cloth, wood, and foam and styrofoam plastics, they tend towards the lifelike and imitative end of the continuum. Similarly, when materials are deployed in a way that calls some attention to them, as is often the case with leather, fibers, buttons, and zippers, their quality has a self-exaggerating aspect, and they tend toward the stylized part of the continuum. And when materials are deployed in a way that insistently calls attention to them, as is often the case with less frequently used materials such as metals, glass, and, interestingly, living flesh, they tend towards the unlifelike, conceptual end of the continuum.

Before we conclude our survey of the major design variables, it will be useful to note a variable that is not generally as significant as those already discussed, and also an aspect of design that should probably not be called a variable in itself, but that can have an important bearing on design.

The variable just referred to is color. In certain traditions, the color of a puppet's face or costume can bear communicative meaning. In the Javanese shadow-theatre, "color is an important indication of mood or emotional state. A puppet with gold *wanda* (face or face and body) indicates dignity and calmness, while black can mean anger or strength. . . . Red indicates tempestuousness or fury. . . . Youth or innocence may be shown by a white face" (Brandon 1970: 50).

General associations of certain colors with certain emotions, such as red with fury, are, no doubt, almost universal. But it seems rare for color to be codified to the degree that it is in the Javanese shadow-theatre, where it has specific, rather than general, connotations. In that it can have such associations, however, and in that it can be subjected to codification, color is another, if not universal, variable of puppet design.

The aspect of design that is not a variable in itself may be called transference, for it involves the transferring of human characteristics to the design of an animal. The Muppets are perhaps the most famous examples of this: Kermit the Frog and Miss Piggy are taken by the audience with no greater or lesser seriousness than are the human puppets Bert and Ernie. It is as if Kermit and Miss Piggy were people who just happened to be animals.

Transference simplifies yet enriches characterization. It simplifies by offering an easily recognizable set of characteristics: if Miss Piggy were portrayed as human, her central characteristic of foolish pretension would require substantial development; but to be pretentious, and to be a pig, is self-evident foolishness. Transference enriches characterization by offering an easily recognizable context. Because Kermit is a frog with an acutely human consciousness, he has the opportunity to reflect upon what it means to be a frog; he can also engage in froglike activity, without forfeiting the audience's sympathy.

Surprisingly, given the pervasiveness of animal folktales and fables, the practice of transference seems to be relatively rare in Eurasian puppet traditions. It should be noted that in traditions such as the Javanese, various gods are represented as animals; but this representation arises from the conventional depiction of certain gods in animal form, and the transference involved is not a function of theatrical choice. The development of transference in theatrical puppetry is a fascinating question: is it inspired by Walt Disney's cartoon animations of such characters as Mickey Mouse and Donald Duck? What then inspired Disney: Victorian children's literature? This question surely extends beyond the domain of puppet aesthetics, and is worthy of wide-ranging research.

At any rate, Jim Henson originally created Kermit not as a frog, but as a "sort of lizardy thing" not intended to represent any particular animal (Henson Associates 1980: 25). Working with designer Don Sahlin, he began to create puppets that were recognizably animals, and Kermit evolved into a frog who remained, nonetheless, peculiarly human (Henson Associates 1980: 8). The example of transference set most obviously by Disney and the Muppets has been followed with tedious regularity by less original artists, and has become a staple of American puppet productions.

John Glore, in a review of the 1980 International Puppetry Festival held in Washington, D.C., remarks:

> Puppetry gratifies our anthropocentric desire to find ourselves in everything. . . . It is no coincidence that puppets so often take the form of humanized animals; this satisfies two of puppetry's central impulses: the personification of an animal, but also, the animalization of humanity, whereby the human world achieves animal innocence and lack of self-consciousness. (1980: 61)

This explanation, if a bit overstated, seems to account for the psychological appeal of human consciousness transferred to animal design. It should be pointed out, however, that the same explanation applies equally to most animal characters in cartoon animation, and, indeed, to most stage animals depicted by masked and costumed actors. As such, it refers to the general practice of transference, rather than to the practice as it occurs specifically in puppetry.

Transference may also be used to instill human characteristics into what are, in the real world, obviously objects. For instance, in our American example, a sofa and a padded chair are among the characters of the opera, given song in the same manner as the other characters, and given movement as well, using their armrests as arms, and dancing a pas de deux of surpassing clumsiness. Transference to real-world objects is less common than it is to animals, but the possibilities for simplification and enrichment of character are similar.

We come at last to the final, and potentially most significant, of the major variables in the puppet's sign-system of design: the on-stage absence or presence of the puppet-operator(s). This is a variable of design because it can have a profound impact upon the way in which the puppet is seen. It is not a variable of movement because, whether the operator is visually absent or present, the movement given to the puppet generally remains unaltered.

Batchelder informs us:

> Practices regarding the concealment of the means by which puppets are controlled vary considerably. Some puppeteers are careful to allow as little as possible of the mechanics to show, but others frankly admit that the puppets are mechanically operated, and they often succeed in creating just as powerful a dramatic illusion. (1947: 185)

The most obvious means of puppet control that can be concealed or exposed is the actual operation of the puppet itself. And beyond doubt, practices regarding the on-stage absence or presence of the operator vary greatly.

The sign of operator absence or presence has a fundamental impact on the quality and quantity of the puppet's design-signs as a whole. When the operator is absent, as in our Nigerian and English examples, the quality of the puppet's design-signs, made up of the variables of features, size, and materials, is presented without visual mediation to the audience; the quantity of design-signs is limited to those of the puppet itself. The directness of such presentation can be of extreme importance: in our Nigerian example, if any of the operators allowed even the mechanics of operation to be revealed, "the whole company was likely to be slain by the spectators. At the very least, the offending puppeteer would be killed" (Malkin 1977: 66).

When the operator is present, however, as in our American, Indian, and Japanese examples, the quality of the puppets' design-signs is immediately transformed, just as the quantity of design-signs is expanded to include the operator's presence. This presence alters the overall design-signs presented on-stage, and, regardless of those of the puppet itself, presents an overall design that is unlifelike in quality and quantity, and is conceptual, in that the visual concept of the puppet as puppet is stressed.

Perhaps the best example of the transforming presence of the operator is the Japanese Bunraku. The puppets themselves present design-signs of nearly lifelike quality and quantity; but with the presence of up to three operators for each puppet, the overall design-sign is wrenched from the imitative, for nothing that is truly lifelike can so obviously be controlled by others. It may well be that the radical juxtaposition of nearly lifelike puppets with the utterly unlifelike presence of their operators accounts for some of the power of Bunraku puppetry: the puppets, regardless of their own imitative design-signs, are made conceptual in a manner that compels the audience to consider the puppets' ontological status. As we have seen, Kott writes of Bunraku's simultaneous "absolute illusion," and "absolute destruction" of that illusion, in which "theatre and metatheatre" are set against each other (1976: 100). Thus, in Bunraku puppetry, signs of design are pushed to the limits of both imitative and conceptual representation, provoking the process of double-vision in perhaps its most extreme form.

Bunraku is not the only puppet theatre that utilizes the on-stage presence of operators. The solo performances of Bruce Schwartz, one of America's finest puppet-artists in recent times, and of Peter Arnott take place with the operator/speaker in full view of the audience. Schwartz, however, says that "I keep the mechanics out in the open because I don't want people to pay attention to them. . . . My theory is that watching me move the puppets with my hands will become dull after a little while. When it does, the puppets will be more interesting than I am" (1983: 106). Arnott comments similarly that "after the first few seconds the audience is oblivious to my presence and concentrates wholly on the [puppet] action" (1964: 81). If these explanations are not taken to be disingenuous, then they must certainly be considered naive: while the performer's on-stage presence renders conceptual the overall design of the puppets, his obvious concentration on his puppets also encourages the audience to accord them imaginary life. Indeed, in the case of Arnott, with his emphasis on producing Greek tragedies, his on-stage presence may be said to lend a metatextual message to the performance: the puppets are, quite literally, under the control of a greater, if not godlike, being.

Contrary to Schwartz and Arnott, then, it would not seem that they, as operators and speakers, "become dull" or that the audience becomes oblivious to them; rather, their on-stage presence must be recognized as a vital aspect of their performances in general.

THE SIGN-SYSTEM OF MOVEMENT

Most puppet-artists have little doubt that the sign-system of movement is the most important of the puppet's three sign-systems. As we have seen, both Baird and McPharlin define the puppet primarily in terms of movement. Obraztsov states, in no uncertain terms:

> The puppet is created to be mobile. Only when it moves does it become alive and only in the character of its movements does it acquire what we call behavior. . . . Of course the text, assuming there is one, has enormous importance, but if the words a puppet speaks do not correspond with its gestures, they become divorced from the puppet and hang in the air. (1950: 125)

Veltruský makes a point about puppet movement that seems remarkable only in that it comes from a semiotician:

> The motions imparted to the puppets are similar to those of the beings they represent. This is not a matter of more or less precise formulation; a crucial moment of the puppet performance is at stake. . . . The puppets' motions convey a meaning of internal impulse corresponding to the impulse that produces the live beings' movements . . . and, by contiguity, this implied meaning reflects in the spectator's mind on the puppets themselves, thus tending to attribute to them life of their own. (1983: 89)

Veltruský is correct that representative movement is "a crucial moment" in puppet performance; most puppet-artists, however, would argue that it is *the* crucial moment.

The argument for the dominance of movement over either design or speech runs as follows. The design of a puppet may be radically unlifelike, presenting the audience with signs so unrepresentative of a given character as to be unintelligible by themselves. The previously mentioned *Aventures* of the Budapest State Puppet Theatre, with its suits and wigs and stoles, is an example of such unlifelike design. Likewise, the speech of a puppet may be radically modified, or the puppet may be given no speech at all, presenting the audience with signs that are either unintelligible or nonexistent: examples of radical modification will be offered in the next section; examples of puppets with no speech would include all puppet-mime and puppet-ballet. But the general movement of the puppet must be intelligible as character movement, or else the design and speech, whatever their representational quality, will be nothing more than plastic art and oratory.

There is an extension of this argument that treats directly the relative importance of movement and speech. The perceived object of the puppet is given movement directly by its operator; that is, it actually moves. The perceived object of the puppet may also be given speech, but it never actually speaks. Thus, movement is intrinsically more important for the puppet than speech. This argument seems justified in light of the widespread performance practice noted by McPharlin: "When two puppets are on stage and one speaks, that puppet must move and the other be still, or else the audience cannot tell which is supposed to be the speaker" (1938: 81). Although movement is often significant in itself, it is also significant for allowing the identification of the speaking puppet; too much movement overwhelms and obliterates the weaker sign-system of speech.

Our concern in this section is to explain the major variables of puppet movement, and to describe how they are used to generate abstracted signs of life along the continuum of representation. These variables include the control mechanics, the control points, and the articulation points of the puppet, and the lighting and scenery that can allow for the implication of puppet movement.

The variables of movement operate in a different manner than those discussed in the previous section. There, each variable contained what might be called a sub-sign-system within the broader sign-system; thus, we were able to address sub-sign-systems such as features, size, and so on. The variables in this sign-system contain no such sub-sign-systems. This difference arises from the static nature of design, as opposed to the dynamic nature of movement. While the variables in design present themselves directly as feature-signs, size-signs, and so on, the variables in movement do not, in themselves, present signs. They operate on a level beneath that of the sign itself; they generate signs of movement.

The first three variables in the sign-system of movement, the control mechanics, the control points, and the articulation points of the puppet, are all intrinsic to the puppet, and are generally subsumed under the term puppet type, as in the object-control taxonomy. McPharlin states that "puppet movement may be classed as movement of type and movement of degree. Each type of puppet, according to its articulation and control, has its characteristic movement. And this movement might be staid or violent, realistic or abstract" (1938: 81). Although this definition recognizes the variables of control mechanics and articulation, it remains limited by a reliance on the general movement characteristics of puppet types. As we have seen, the actual number of types is quite uncertain, and even within established types, movement-signs can differ drastically. It is impossible, for example, to characterize hand-puppet movement as simply and always violent. Hand-puppets happen to be very good at hyperactive movement, but they might also be moved in a careful and deliberate manner. Likewise, it is impossible to characterize marionette movement as simply and always staid. Marionettes, at least of the string variety, happen to be very good at slow and stately movement; but they may also be swung around with great force.

Our purpose in breaking down the discussion of puppet types into three separate intrinsic variables is to allow for a more accurate and detailed description of the manner in which puppets generate movement-signs. First, control mechanics are the means by which the operator exerts control; second, control points are those places on the puppet at which the control is exerted; and third, articulation points are those places where the puppet is jointed to allow for differential movement of its parts. To understand how these variables operate, it will be best to examine a few of the standard puppet types.

The control mechanics for the traditional Western string marionette are the strings, held by the operator, from which the puppet hangs. Puppet movement derives from the opposing forces of the operator's pull on the strings and the counteropposed pull of gravity; the movement of a string creates either a rising and falling puppet movement, or a pendular puppet movement. Rising and falling movement, such as a puppet hand sawing in the air, or a head nodding in agreement, is generated regardless of string length. The operator pulls on a string at a certain speed, and the commensurate rising movement is performed at that speed; when the operator relaxes tension, the falling movement occurs at a speed no greater than the pull of gravity.

For pendular movement, such as a puppet hand reaching out toward an object, or legs swung in a walk, string length is an important consideration. McPharlin notes that "the longer the string, the smaller the arc of pendulous movement at its end, and the more human-appearing the action of a properly weighted figure" (1938: 85). Or, to view the matter from a different perspective, the longer the string, the slower and finer the resultant pendular movement. Whatever the string length, the operator pulls a string in a certain direction, and a part or the whole of the puppet is set swinging. This swinging ends when its pendular potential is exhausted, or when the operator pulls the string back, or when the moving part of the puppet is grounded by friction, as in the steps a marionette takes while walking.

The control mechanics of strings operated from above have a number of consequences. For example, string marionettes have a natural ability to fly, as the operator's upward pull on the strings can easily overcome the downward pull of gravity. They cannot, however, grasp objects, for while their hands may be swung together, they cannot be made to apply pressure; this limitation can, however, be obviated to a degree through the use of such devices as hooks and velcro. Also, marionettes cannot "run" well, for although their legs can be lifted up quickly enough, they cannot be lowered back to the ground any faster than the pull of gravity. The only way to have a marionette "run" is to hide the legs with a long skirt or gown, or abandon any pretense to imitative movement and just whisk it along with as much leg movement as possible.

The control mechanics for the traditional Western hand-puppet, such as Punch in our English performance example, are far simpler than those of the string marionette: they are but the hand and fingers of the operator on which the puppet is set. In general, hand-puppet movement derives directly from the movement of the operator's hand and fingers. There are no elaborate calculations to be made, as with the string marionette, concerning rising and falling forces, or pendular action, or the distance between the operator and the puppet. The hand-puppet is, as we have seen earlier, nothing more or less than a costume, with whatever elaboration, for the human hand held in an upright posture. This intimacy of control mechanics offers the hand-puppet an immediate responsiveness to control that is absent in the marionette, allowing it the fast and furious movement often noted as its primary characteristic. It should not be thought, however, that hand-puppet movement is limited to broad humor: in the Chinese tradition of Fujian Province, for example, hand-puppet movement can attain a remarkable level of stylized precision, with puppets presenting martial arts combat of astonishing drama and detail (Stalberg 1984: 33–34).

The consequences of the hand-puppet's control mechanics are quite different than those of the string marionette. For example, the hand-puppet is generally incapable of flight, as the hand can be raised only so far before the bottom of the puppet becomes visible, and, beneath that, the arm of the operator. Even if the operator is present on-stage with the puppet, no sense of flight can be sustained, owing to the puppet's obvious connection, through the arm and body of the operator, with the ground. A rare exception is in the Fujian Province tradition, in which puppets are tossed up into the air and caught again, "with no break in dramatic rhythm" (Stalberg 1984: 34); but this spectacular movement greatly differs from the sustained flight of which the marionette is capable. The hand-puppet can easily grasp objects, however, as the operator is able to create a pincer-like force between the fingers in the puppet's arms. And the hand-puppet is the "running" puppet par excellence: in most cases, its legs and feet are simply assumed to be beneath the playing level, and the puppet need merely be given a rapid up and down twisting motion as it "runs" across the stage; in other cases, it might indeed have legs, given direct movement by the operator's second hand.

The control points for a string marionette are those places at which the strings are attached to the puppet. In many contemporary Western marionettes, the control points would include one on each side of the head, one on each shoulder, one on the rear end, as well as one on each hand and one on each knee or foot (Baird 1965: 161). The control points are important in determining the movement possibilities of the puppet. For example, control points on the sides of the head, as opposed to a single such point on the top of the head, allow for the head to be pivoted from side to side, as well as up and down, although the control mechanics and the articulation of the puppet remain unchanged.

Of course, there can be a larger number of control points, for the sake of specialized movements; each finger may, for instance, be a control point for a piano-playing marionette. There can also be fewer control points, as we have seen in our Indian example, in which each puppet has only four—the head and the rear end, and the two hands (Baird 1965: 47).

The control points for the hand-puppet are those places where the pressure of the operator's fingers and hand is applied to the puppet. The conventional hand-puppet has three such points: the ends of the puppet's arms and the puppet's head. By exertion of pressure on these three points, almost all hand-puppet movement is generated.

The number of control points for the hand-puppet is only slightly variable. An additional such point can be created by folding one or two of the operator's fingers in the puppet's chest or belly; this is useful for generating the specialized movement of a pounding heart or a kicking fetus. Any of the three standard control points can be left unattended, but all that this does is generate movement of a deformed nature.

Contemporary Western marionettes generally have articulation points mirroring the major articulation points of the human body. James Juvenal Hayes, an American puppet-artist in the first part of this century, believed that "fifteen joints are ideal . . . ; they would be at each end of the neck, the shoulders, elbows, wrists, hips, knees, and ankles" (quoted in McPharlin 1938: 79). These articulation points are also important in determining the movement possibilities of the puppet. For example, articulation points at the hips and the knees, as opposed to such points at the hips alone, allow for differential movement of the upper and lower legs, as well as for differential movement of the leg as a whole, although the control mechanics and the control points of the puppet remain unchanged.

And, of course, the number of articulation points in the marionette is variable. The piano-playing puppet suggested above would require an articulation point at the base of each finger. Conversely, there may be fewer, as in our Indian example, in which no articulation points are provided at the elbows, the whole of the arm being "made from a fabric that is stuffed with a springy, fibrous substance" that allows for a more generalized bending (Malkin 1977: 75).

The articulation points of the hand-puppet are far fewer than those of the marionette, existing at the points where the human hand has its major articulations. Thus, articulation points exist at the neck and shoulders of the hand-puppet, where the operator's fingers are articulated at the joint that connects them to the palm, and at the puppet's waist, where the operator's hand is articulated at the wrist. This last articulation is surprisingly expressive. McPharlin remarks that the wrist "has the same rotary and far-forward, not-so-far backward bend as the human waist. This makes kowtowing, working over a washboard, swinging an ax, and other movements hinging from the waist particularly *vraisemblable* in a hand-puppet" (1938: 89). An additional articulation point can be created in the puppet's chest or belly, as mentioned earlier, because the body of the hand-puppet is generally constructed of a malleable material. And of course, any of these articulation points may be left unused.

This examination of the three intrinsic variables in the marionette and the hand-puppet suggests how they work separately and together to generate movement. Almost all puppet movement is derived from these variables, and is describable in terms of them. It will be recalled that, in his discussion of traditional shadow-puppets, Baird notes differences in the manner in which the control rods are connected to the puppets. Let us conclude our analysis of the three intrinsic variables with an examination of those differences in some detail.

In both Greek and Javanese shadow-puppets, the control mechanics are rods: in the former, only a single rod is generally used, with occasional puppets being controlled by two (Baird 1965: 79); in the latter, three rods are generally employed (Brandon 1970: 51). Thus according to the object-control taxonomy, while both are shadow-puppets, both are also rod-puppets: "By definition, the shadow-figure *is* a rod-puppet" (Batchelder 1947: xix). Their movements, however, are distinctly different, as Baird reports. The differences arise from the different number of rods employed, and from the differing control points and articulation points.

The single control point of most Greek shadow-puppets is a hole in the upper body, into which the support rod is inserted at a right angle.

The figure was, traditionally, nailed to the rod; but according to Sotiris Spatharis, the most highly acclaimed of Greek Karaghioz puppet-artists, in 1924 the art was "revolutionized" by the use of a hinge in place of the nail, "making it possible for the figure to change direction, face-about" (1976 [1960]: 128). These hinges, one per puppet, are generally located at the edge of the puppet's rear shoulder, the puppet being presented in profile; with a jerk of the control rod, the puppet is pulled away from the screen and pivoted on the hinge to face in the other direction. Whether using the nail or the hinge, the operator must maintain a hold on the control rod throughout the performance. A second control point exists for certain puppets, for a moveable arm or phallus (Myrsiades 1988: 28–29). When two puppets are on-stage, neither can have an active second rod. Further, Spatharis informs us that, despite exaggerated reports, no performer "can hold and manipulate more than two figures at a time" (1976 [1960]: 141).

The control points for Javanese shadow-puppets differ greatly. An extended point exists along the puppet's spine, from which the rod descends downward to the operator; the puppet can easily be turned around, and can be kept on-stage indefinitely with its support rod thrust into a banana-wood log beneath the stage-level, freeing the hand of the operator. Two additional rods connect to control points at the puppet's hands, and can be left to dangle freely. Thus, an array of puppets can be on-stage at any given time, gesticulating to one another (Brandon 1970: 51–63).

The articulation points used in the two traditions of shadow-puppets also differ. For the Greek puppets, Malkin counts "three or four joints," with "one at the waist, a second and third at each knee, and a fourth [for puppets with a second rod] at one of the elbows" (1977: 62). As there are no control points below the waist, the articulation points at the waist and the knees are used to give a free-swinging quality to the puppet's walk. The articulation point at the elbow, if present, allows for a simple flexing of the lower part of the arm.

In the Javanese tradition, while there are still generally only four articulation points, they are dedicated exclusively to enabling arm movement for the puppet, the points being at each shoulder and each elbow (Baird 1965: 57). As there are no articulation points on the legs, puppets are made to "walk" by their entire bodies being bobbed up and down in various stylized ways. Once a puppet is settled on-stage, the operator may then have it "tie [its] sash, fix [its] headgear, or stroke [its] moustache," or so on, to establish its character (Brandon 1970: 65). In the course of the scene, the articulation points allow the arms detailed gesticulation, "bringing the rear arm sharply forward from the face" for greeting, "draping the forearm over the shoulder" for sorrow, and so on (Brandon 1970: 66). Articulated movement might be limited to the arms, but, with two articulation points for each, the possible range of such movement, in quality and quantity, is superior to that of the Greek shadow-puppet.

We may conclude, following from this examination, that Greek and Javanese shadow-puppets have remarkably different movement possibilities, arising precisely from their differences in control points and articulation points. No categorization based on their historic-geographic tradition or object-control classification as shadow- or rod-puppets can convey their distinctive attributes of movement.

There is yet one more variable in puppet movement, although it operates in a manner completely different than the first three variables, being not intrinsic to the puppet, but extrinsic: lighting and scenery can be used to generate "implicit" movement in the puppet in the absence of actual movement.

McPharlin suggests that "it is movement, actual or illusory, which gives the puppet animation. . . . Indeed, as the face of a puppet moves through zones of light and shadow, the features take on mobility" (1938: 76, 81). The illusory, or implicit, movement of the puppet's facial features, generated by the puppet's movement through light and shadow, can also be generated while the puppet remains stationary, with the light and shadow moving instead.

In shadow theatre, one of the basic movements of the shadow, at least in performances not lit by electric light, derives from movement not of the puppet, but of the light source. As in our Javanese example, "the shadow cast is distinct for a relatively short distance only, but because of the moving and waving flame [of the light source] it seems infused with life" (Brandon 1970: 35). Indeed, the light source itself may be moved from one point to another, causing the shadow of the puppet to move while the puppet remains stationary; again, the movement would not be of the puppet itself, but implied for the puppet. It might be argued that such implied movement would be visible only to those on the far side of the shadow-screen, and thus, available only to shadow-theatre. But, as in McPharlin's suggestion, a puppet directly subjected to a moving and wavering light, to shifting fields of light and shadow, also generates the implication of movement.

For an example of implicit movement, let us turn to the visitor's center on Temple Square in Salt Lake City, where the Latter-Day Saints have used nonmoving figures set against a diorama to relate the stories of their religion, with a tape system supplying narration and character voices. The various figures are highlighted when "speaking"; through the use of subtle lighting effects, the expressions on their faces seem to change, and their hands even seem to gesture. Also, the dioramas themselves are in some cases mobile, and the shifting of their scenes in the background implicitly suggests movement of the figures through space.

As we have seen with double-vision, puppetry is a function of audience perception and imagination; the puppet need not, literally, be an object, and it cannot, literally, be alive. Likewise, signs of puppet movement need not, literally, be generated by movement of the puppet itself; they can be generated from outside, giving the implication of movement. Whatever the literal generation of the movement, it is perceived by the audience as puppet movement, and, as with the puppet's abstracted signs in general, it helps provoke the imagination of life.

It remains to be demonstrated how the movement-signs generated by the major variables, three intrinsic and one extrinsic to the puppet, might be located along the continuum of representation. In the chart given earlier, the three stages of representative signs were labelled as with, despite, and against the puppet. Movement-signs made with the puppet are signs for whose deployment the intrinsic variables have been expressly created; these signs provide a quality of imitative representation. Movement-signs made despite the puppet are signs for whose deployment the intrinsic variables have not been expressly created, but of which they are nonetheless somewhat capable; these signs provide a quality of conventional and stylized representation. Movement-signs made against the puppet are signs for whose deployment the intrinsic variables have little or no relevance, and in which the extrinsic variable might be used to generate implicit movement; these signs provide a quality of conceptual representation. In all cases, the quantity of movement-signs is simply the sum of the generated movements.

An example of movement-signs made with the puppet is our Japanese example: the puppets give detailed signs of walking and gesturing, and even of "crying, heavy breathing, sewing, smoking, and dancing" (Adachi 1985: 51). The quality and quantity of these signs are generated by the control mechanics, which are short rods, often with triggers for specialized movement, as well as direct hand-to-puppet contact; by the control points, at the base of the head, the ends of the forearms, and the feet, as well as those places operated by the triggered controls, such as the eyebrows and the fingers; and by the articulation points, which closely mirror those of the human body.

Such complexity, however, is not required for movement with the puppet. Stefan Lenkisch, producer of a Romanian puppet theatre, relates his discovery that "if [the] puppet performed one particular movement to perfection the spectator would gain the impression that it could perform any conceivable movement" (1967 [1965]: 28). Simplicity can be as effective in its own way as complexity. One movement, toward the perfection of which the intrinsic variables are created — such as the supple wave of a hand, with the wrist flexing and the fingers spreading out — is enough to set the audience to imagining a fully rounded life of movement for the puppet.

Simplicity and complexity may also be intertwined ingeniously, as in this example given by Obraztsov:

> To make a puppet which can perform all the physical movements of a human being is impossible. One cannot, for example, make a puppet able to shave, bathe, jump from a height, sail a yacht, dance a waltz and do handstands. . . . The hero of our play *Two-Love to Us* has to do all these in the course of the plot. That is why we have had to make a series of puppets, which appear outwardly the same but whose anatomical structure varies. The spectator's impression is that he has seen only one puppet throughout the whole play. In fact, there are thirty of them. (1954: 13)

An example of movement-signs made despite the puppet can be found in our Javanese shadow-puppet performance. As we have seen, these puppets have no articulation points below the waist, yet they "walk" on and off the stage. This walk, with fixed and immobile legs, is accepted by convention, for the construction of the puppet does not allow for any manner of walking that is not stylized. Despite this, the walks of various characters are quite distinguishable, owing to the operator's control of the support and arm rods. For instance, "Ardjuna walks smoothly across the screen, with no vertical movement. Both arms hang straight down or one swings back and forth gently. . . . Bima bounds across the screen in two or three leaps, rear arm cocked behind him and forearm raised high in a strong gesture" (Brandon 1970: 65).

Another case of movement-signs made despite the puppet can be found in our English example of Punch. As we have seen, while the operator's wrist allows for great articulation at the waist of the puppet, the same cannot be said for the fingers in the puppet's arms. The movement of the puppet's arms derives solely from the articulation points at its shoulders, and the arms, incapable of bending at the elbows, are always stiff (McPharlin 1938: 89). This movement is stylized, and is accepted conventionally as the appropriate arm movement of the hand-puppet.

It should be noted that movement-signs made despite the puppet must maintain, in their stylization and conventionalization, a certain consistency of representation. Rose Soroky, in a generally superficial look at puppet aesthetics, writes, "The audience cannot empathize with a puppet whose feet do not touch the ground or whose knees are bent when he walks" (1982: 6). In fact, the audience can indeed empathize, but only if the convention is established and maintained that none of the puppets' feet touch the ground, or that, as in our Javanese example, every puppets' knees are bent.

An example of movement-signs made against the puppet was given in our discussion of the Salt Lake City production, in which lighting and scenery generated implicit movement. But movement against the puppet is not limited to implicit movement. It occurs whenever the puppet is treated as the object that the audience perceives it to be.

In the Javanese shadow-theatre,

> Supernatural characters can be made to grow in size by bringing the
> puppet closer to the lamp. An extremely beautiful effect is created by
> moving a puppet slowly to the edge of the playing area while with-
> drawing it from the screen, then bringing it back on again. The shadow
> dissolves and vanishes in the air, then rematerializes. . . . A special effect
> is produced when a figure is turned to face in the opposite direction: it
> looks as if the character compresses into a thin line, then expands out-
> ward again. (Brandon 1970: 36)

These movement-signs are generated with a total disregard for the articulation of the puppet. The control mechanics and control points are
involved only in that they allow the operator to treat the puppet as an
object susceptible to general movement. Yet these movements are especially pleasing and provocative.

In battle-scenes in the Liège tradition, "whenever a large figure representing a general, and six or seven small figures collided, often in
midair, with a similar group, audience members understood that they
were witnessing a titanic battle" (Malkin 1977: 25). The audience was
actually witnessing puppets being given movement as if they were little
else but projectile objects; again, no articulation is necessary for such
movement, and no special control points. All that matters is that the
operators have a means to fling the puppets into battle.

Movement against the puppet is relatively rare, but it demonstrates
how movement-signs, just as design-signs, can span the full range of
the continuum of representation, provoking double-vision in any number of ways.

THE SIGN-SYSTEM OF SPEECH

Speech, everyone seems to agree, is different. We have seen how
Veltruský suggests that the sign-system of speech differs from the
others because, in it, "the *signans* and the *signatum* are existentially the
same" (1983: 71); we have also seen how Green and Pepicello locate it

in its own "auditory" channel, separate from the "visual" channel shared by design and movement (1983: 147). The significance of the difference between speech and movement is, however, the subject of profound disagreement. We have seen how Baird and McPharlin utterly disregard speech in their definitions of the puppet, and how Obraztsov cavalierly dispenses with "the text, assuming there is one" (1950: 120). Now we must discuss how certain scholars have come to consider speech to be the most important sign-system of the puppet.

Samuel Foote, a nineteenth-century English theatre-artist and producer, tells this story about the Roman orator Livius Andronicus:

> Upon delivering a popular sentiment in one of his pieces, [he] was so often encored that, quite exhausted, he declared himself incapable of a further repetition, unless one of his scholars was permitted to mount the stage, and suffered to declaim the passage, which he [Livius] would attempt to gesticulate. . . . Here, gentlemen, by separation of the personage, you have the puppet complete. (1812: 150)

The piece containing this story is shot through with assertions concerning ancient theatre, many of them no less remarkable. Jurkowski comments, with an almost apologetic air: "Leaving aside the historical aspect of Foote's statement, we must admit that he pointed at the essential feature of the puppet theatre" (1988 [1983]: 74). He goes on to affirm that "the separability of the speaking object and the physical source of the word . . . is the distinctive feature of the puppet theatre" (1988 [1983]: 79).

Despite Jurkowski's affirmation, Foote's assertion seems so extreme as to be foolish. Are we really to take Livius Andronicus, with his flesh and blood gesticulations, to be a puppet? Obviously he is not: he is not an object in the inanimate sense used by most writers, including Jurkowski; neither is he an "object" in the expanded sense used in this study. He is, quite clearly, a living man, miming the delivery of a speech actually spoken by another.

Jurkowski does not seem to have articulated an argument for the singular importance of the separation of "speaking object" and "physical source of the word," and it is possible that he does not quite mean what he says. In another article, he writes: "In any theory of puppet theatre, the most important factor is the relationship between puppeteer and puppet" (1988 [1979]: 4). As we have seen, his own definition of the puppet theatre takes pains to highlight the variability of this relationship, not only for speech, but for movement as well. Perhaps, inspired by Foote, he simply has gone overboard in focusing on the relationship in terms of speech.

Veltruský does not want to go as far as Jurkowski seems to go in claiming the predominance of speech: "The [general] sign produced in puppetry neither automatically counteracts the predominance of the verbal, literary component . . . nor favor[s] such a predominance" (1983: 97). This seems even-handed enough, but, in the same article, Veltruský makes his own remarkable assertion for the power of puppet speech. In ventriloquism, he suggests:

> It is by its own particular sound qualities that the ventriloquist's way of speaking—an impeded way—calls forth the image of the speaker as human-like but not quite human; with the help of this convention, this human-like speaker is perceived as a dummy. This is true even when the voice performance stands alone, as in the case of the popular radio performance of Peter Brough and his dummy Archie Andrews on the BBC in the 1950's. It is perhaps not too far-fetched a conclusion that the strange delivery of a ventriloquist or a puppeteer with a voice modifier conveys a corresponding image of the dummy or puppet in any event. (1983: 103)

If this is, indeed, "not too far-fetched," then signs from the sign-system of speech alone are sufficient to constitute the puppet. And if they are, then surely speech is the most important sign-system of the puppet. But is it not too far-fetched? It is likely that the radio audience of Peter Brough, or similarly, of Edgar Bergen in America, is aware, through previous knowledge, of the existence of the puppets Archie Andrews or Charlie McCarthy, and that their attribution of speech to them, as puppets, is a function of this previous knowledge, and not of the speech delivery alone. That is, the speech delivery reinforces the knowledge that there is an unseen puppet, but does not constitute the puppet by itself. If the radio audience were not aware that a puppet was "speaking," it seems it would simply take that speech to be appropriate to a particular character. And so, despite Veltruský's suggestion, signs of speech, by themselves, cannot be considered to have the power to constitute the puppet.

But still, it might be argued, the different nature of the sign-system of speech gives it overwhelming importance in puppetry. Erik Kolár suggests that the "inanimate material of the puppet and the puppeteer's human voice," while seeming to be at odds, actually "constitute a specific and dialectic unity in puppet theatre: the synthesis of live voice and animated puppet" (1964: 68). Bogatyrev assents to this suggestion, and goes on to assert that "the puppet seems more alive when its movements are combined with a human voice. In a performance where the puppets merely pantomime, the animation of the puppet's inanimate matter without a human voice accompanying its movements is not as convincing to the spectator" (1983 [1973]: 60). Kolár and Bogatyrev seem to assume that puppet speech is more or less human-sounding in its delivery, and that it is directly attributed to the puppet. Even when this is the case, as in our African example, and in much contemporary American puppetry, this "dialectical unity" provided by speech is problematic. One might argue, to the contrary, that human-sounding speech attributed to the puppet undermines the puppet's presumption of "life" by setting in unhappy contrast the artificiality of its design and movement.

Moreover, the presuppositions of Kolár and Bogatyrev are themselves problematic. In our English and Indian examples, puppet speech is modified to such a degree that it has few of the characteristics of human speech. In our Japanese example, speech for all of the characters is delivered by a visible speaker, while in our American example, it is delivered by visible singers: in both cases, it is clearly separated from the puppet. The relationship of voice to puppet is far more complex than Kolár and Bogatyrev seem to acknowledge. Jurkowski's complaint against synchronic reductionism surely applies here.

But it remains to be said that speech is, indeed, different, and in three ways. First, alone among the three sign-systems, it is, in fact, dispensable, and is fairly often dispensed with.

For example: in 1983, the Pandemonium Puppet Company pre-

sented a sketch called "Frog and Blocks," directed by Bart Roccoberton, Jr. An anthropomorphic frog, no relation to Kermit, comes
on-stage oblivious of the audience. He sweeps the play-board, which
has been liberally sprinkled with baby powder, into a dust-storm; the
audience laughs, and the frog realizes he is not alone. Although the audience expects the frog to speak, he remains silent. He bows, shows
frustration at the tepid response he is given, and bows again to a greater
response. As he continues toying with the audience, a playing-block
slides on-stage, and the frog trips over it as he returns to his dusting.
He moves it aside and returns again to his work; it slides back behind
him and he trips over it again.

The sketch continues in silence, with two additional blocks eventually appearing, for a full five minutes. It may well be that the tension
created by the frog's silence is an important factor in the success of the
piece, for his lack of speech leaves the audience hanging on his every
movement: a twitch of his head or a shrug of his shoulders communicates his character more clearly than might any speech.

A sketch of this sort is not without limitations; most especially, the
lack of speech is difficult to sustain without the tension it creates dissi-
pating into audience frustration. Jiří Trnka, a Czech film-maker who
used puppets to beautiful effect, included no puppet speech in his first
movies, but eventually found value in it:

> After [Trnka's] experiences when filming Old Czech Legends, to which
> [limited puppet dialogue] had added such a powerful effect, he could not
> resist the temptation to develop it further. He now realized that he
> needed to make his puppets speak in order to infuse new life into them.
> Prior to this film he had used words only with caution. . . . In Old
> Czech Legends, he used them in a much more complicated and exacting
> manner. A dignified monologue introduced in the form of an outside
> commentary had considerable impact, and in addition to this, the pup-
> pets themselves spoke several times. This left Trnka only a small [step]
> from expansion into more dialogue, with all the added attraction of
> fuller characterization and entertaining repartee. (Bocek 1963: 191)

Puppet speech can certainly offer "fuller characterization and entertain-
ing repartee," as well as the expression of profound and literary dialogue. But clearly, whatever it might add to puppet performance, it is

in no way required for it. As such, it is impossible to agree with those who claim that speech is, in one way or another, "the distinctive feature of the puppet theatre."

The second way in which speech is different from the other sign-systems is that it can be presented automatically, without affecting the audience's sense of the puppet as perceived object and imagined life. This is most commonly done, with growing frequency in America, by playing a tape recording of the sound track in correspondence with the physical performance of the puppets. We need not discuss at length the aesthetic effects of using "canned" dialogue: suffice it to say that, on the one hand, the production gains a certain regularity of competent vocal performance, with which musical accompaniment and sound effects can be well integrated, while, on the other hand, all spontaneity of performance is lost to the unvarying pace of the recording.

This matter of prerecorded dialogue is especially interesting in that it would seem to be the speech equivalent of mechanical or electronic control of movement. As we have seen, in the latter case we prefer to speak of the mechanically controlled theatrical figure as an automaton, rather than as a puppet. Yet prerecorded dialogue does not seem to raise as vital an issue, in that no writer on puppetry has ever claimed that its use renders the theatrical figure something other than a puppet, though many deplore it for the loss of spontaneity it engenders. It may well be that this is just another way in which puppet speech is, at least tacitly, considered to be less important than puppet movement.

The third way in which speech differs from the other sign-systems is that, as Veltruský, Bogatyrev, Green, and Pepicello, as well as others have noted, it is more grounded in real life than they are, generally being produced by a human voice signifying a human voice. As suggested earlier, this difference can work to the benefit or the detriment of the puppet performance; but the puppet-artist who ignores it risks a terrible inconsistency in the deployment of signs. Discussing his early failures in attributing speech to the puppet, Obraztsov remarks: "I [should] have understood that it is not a question of voice alone but of the need for the actor's emotions [and voice] to coincide with the puppet's; even with its size" (1950: 119).

This third difference is at the heart of the sign-system of speech, and the variables in the sign-system are all concerned with finding ways in which the puppet's speech may be made to coincide with the puppet's design and movement, to be appropriate to the puppet. The major variables within this sign-system are paralinguistic features, dialect/language, voice modification, and the on-stage presence or absence of the living speaker(s). These variables can act as signs in themselves, as do the variables in the sign-system of design, or as generators of signs, as do the variables in the sign-system of movement.

The first variable involves paralinguistic features, or alternately, suprasegmental features. Elam defines these as "vocal characteristics with which [the speaker] endows [speech] over and above its phonemic and syntactic structure" (1980: 79). Basing his discussion on the work of many linguists, Elam isolates the elements of "loudness, pitch, timbre, rate, inflection, rhythm, and enunciation" (1980: 81). As employed in puppetry, standard combinations of paralinguistic features offer a means of vocal stereotyping that can suggest particular personality traits for various characters while allowing for easily comprehended distinctions between those characters. These combinations of paralinguistic features may be deployed in a manner that approximates normal character speech, presenting speech signs that are imitative in quality and quantity; or they may be deployed in a manner that amounts to caricature of normal speech, presenting speech-signs that are stylized in quality and quantity.

The use of paralinguistic features for the deployment of normal character speech requires little discussion. Every person has his or her own unique vocal attributes; in puppetry, paralinguistic features are combined to create characters with their own unique vocal attributes. One need only walk the streets of any major city to realize how vast is the range of human speech, and with what facility and regularity paralinguistic features are combined.

Paralinguistic features are heavily relied on in our Javanese example. The puppet-operator must deliver not only the speech of numerous characters, but also ritual descriptions and basic narration. Speech differentiation is accomplished through variations of vocal pitch and quality for individual characters; an especially stylized delivery, punctuated by an occasional "sharp rap or two," is employed for ritual descriptions;

and basic narration is spoken plainly, having few "special techniques" associated with it (Brandon 1970: 62–63).

In the Sicilian tradition, there is more than one speaker, but paralinguistic features are nonetheless employed to create stylized representation of speech-signs for various character-types:

> The timbre of the voice changes with the type of character. . . . The positive comic characters . . . speak with nasal, clucking, raucous voices, different from the negative comic characters, who speak dialect with a throaty, strident voice. . . . The positive heroes have a clear, resounding timbre; the negative ones an obscure, throaty and raucous one. (Pasqualino 1987: 11)

It might be noted, with Pasqualino, that in addition to paralinguistic features, the Sicilian tradition also makes use of the dialect/language variable to characterize and distinguish between characters. As in all three sign-systems, the variables may be combined in many ways.

The variable of dialect/language is commonly employed in traditions where class and nationality, as represented by the use of various dialects and languages, are significant attributes of the characters. Also, the use of language by a given character may be so individualized that it amounts to a personal dialect.

After his brilliant survey of voice modification techniques, to which we will soon turn our attention, Proschan discusses three other techniques available to the traditional folk-puppeteer for distinguishing between various characters' speech, and for distinguishing puppet speech from live speech. First, "the solution [in Sicilian puppetry] may be as simple as the shifting of registers from Italian to Sicilian and back for villains and heroes" (1981: 552). As we have seen, paralinguistic features are also a part of the Sicilian solution. Second, the solution may involve "mangled syntax." As Bogatyrev notes, "Old [Czech] puppeteers, conveying the language of upper class heroes . . . , distorted common colloquial language [and] intentionally made grammar mistakes, while puppets depicting peasants spoke Czech correctly" (quoted in Proschan 1981: 552). It seems likely that in other traditions, in which performance was intended for the upper classes, the signs of mangled versus correct speech would be inverted. The third solution involves "exaggerated parodies of stereotypical speaking styles, elaborated far beyond what is necessary to differentiate the characters" (1981: 552). This solution makes use of paralinguistic features, as discussed above.

The most often remarked upon variable in the puppet's sign-system of speech is that of voice modification, in which the voice of the speaker is subjected to modification, or distortion, through the employment of a mechanical device in or at the mouth of the speaker. Proschan offers a summary of devices typically used in traditional puppetry:

> Voice modifiers fall into three groups: those held in the back of the mouth (usually two hard plates bound together with a vibrating ribbon between them); those held in the front of the mouth (these also use a vibrating reed); and those held outside the mouth (these are tube kazoos). (1981: 533)

A voice modifier held in the back of the mouth, between the speaker's upper tongue and palate, called a "swazzle," is used in our English example; one held in the front of the mouth, between the speaker's teeth, is used in our Indian example (Proschan 1981: 534). Voice modifiers held outside the mouth, secured by a harness, include not only the kazoo, but also duck calls and bird whistles, and are not uncommon in contemporary productions.

As this variety of devices suggests, the use of voice modification is not all the same. The further back in the mouth the device is located, the more difficulty the speaker has in articulating the speech. What's more, given any particular device, the speaker still has control over the delivery of speech-signs. Proschan remarks that "in using the voice modifier, the puppeteer can aim for easy intelligibility, for absolute inscrutability, or for some midpoint. The goal varies from one tradition to another, in fact, from one moment to another within the performance" (1981: 533). It would be safe to suggest, however, that voice modification generally produces speech-signs that tend toward the conceptual end of the continuum of representation, for it is the concept of speech, rather than the content, that is attributed to the puppet.

To this list of traditional voice modifying devices must be added those made available by contemporary technology. Whether the performance is "live," delivered through microphones, or on prerecorded tape, electronics offers an array of speech-sign possibilities, including echo effects, aural distortion, and the sheer manipulation of volume, among many others. Generally speaking, these possibilities are not used to create a high degree of unintelligibility, but it would seem that they might be used with as much variety as are traditional voice modification devices.

Unintelligible speech-signs, however produced, are, of course, of limited utility for conveying meaning. How might voice-modified speech be rendered intelligible to the audience? According to Proschan, this can be accomplished in three ways: first, through "dialogue and repetition," in which the puppet's distorted words are clearly repeated in assertive or interrogatory form by an interlocutor, another puppet, or by the puppeteer; second, through "the communicative event," in which puppet movement, such as gesture and action, clarifies the intent of the speech; and third, through the modified speech itself, in which the "close correspondence between the contours of natural speech and the contours of [modified] puppet speech" must be noted, and in which the "redundance and resistance to distortion" of natural speech leaves the puppet's speech full of communicative signification (1981: 535–39).

Voice-modified speech presents obvious burdens to the puppet-artist and the audience, yet it is commonly used in many diverse traditions. The burdens it presents are offset by the benefits it offers. Proschan suggests one of the primary benefits: "A puppeteer who must speak for several puppets has only one natural voice, so he must either rely to a [great] extent on the speech stereotypes, or he must find some other way to alter radically his natural voice (or utilize the two solutions together)" (1981: 528).

Proschan mentions other benefits as well: "The distinctive sound of the voice modifier alerts the audience to the arrival of the puppeteers and the beginning of the performance"; "the squeaky voice is inherently funny"; the voice modifier "can be used for 'secret' communication (the transmission of cues)"; and the voice modifier "can mark when particular characters are speaking," such as when, in their plays, only Punch and Petrushka have modified voices (1981: 540–41). He goes on to say:

> Puppet voices are sometimes explained, even by the same analyst, in opposite terms: they are small voices to correspond to the diminutive size of the puppets . . . yet they are also capable of producing humorous effect by virtue of their incongruity. . . . The truth is that both are correct. . . . We sometimes see an internally consistent, mutually reinforcing semiotic system at work. . . . We sometimes see . . . the interaction of two distinct yet related [systems]. (Proschan 1981: 548–49)

But there is a difference between "small voices" and modified voices. A small voice might correspond to the puppet while not being humorous in itself, as in the gentle yet stylized voice of the Muppets' Kermit; a modified voice might be funny while not corresponding to the puppet, as in the hypothetical case of a swazzle being used for a greater-than-life-size giant in *Jack and the Beanstalk*.

Proschan is attempting to come to terms with what is perhaps the most important benefit of voice modification, a benefit so obvious that he does not explicitly consider it. As Speaight reminds us:

> There is an inherent disparity between the figure of the puppet and the voice of a man; we may become accustomed to the convention by which a full sized human voice is supposed to proceed from the (usually) immobile lips of a marionette, but there is ample evidence that in the past it was considered necessary to disguise the human voice when it spoke in the puppet show. . . . We may well learn . . . that the use of some kind of megaphone or sounding box would lend just that "unhuman" timbre to the voice that is necessary to make the puppet show a completely distinct form of entertainment. (1947: 37–39)

The use of voice modification takes away the "disparity between the figure of the puppet and the voice of a man"; it lends the " 'unhuman' timbre" to the puppet's voice that makes it uniquely its own.

Veltrusky makes much the same point: "In order to combine human speech with the inanimate object and the notion carried out by its means, the delivery is made so strange as to be perceived as the puppet's own voice and the impeded speech as its own speech, anthropomorphous rather than human" (1983: 103). Or, to put in the terms of this study, the ontologically paradoxical puppet is given, with voice modification, an appropriately paradoxical speech.

Because signs of speech are not directly presented by the puppet itself, as are signs of design and movement, the fundamental problem presented to the puppet-artist is that of making the signs of speech seem appropriate. Character speech-signs — speech-signs toward the imitative end of the continuum of representation — are, in much traditional and most contemporary puppet theatre, generally not deployed owing to their lack of appropriateness. Even if only paralinguistic features of speech are used, for the creation of caricature speech, they help to correlate speech with the puppet's other sign-systems. The recurrence of voice modification suggests the degree to which this need for correlation exists.

The last of the variables in the puppet's sign-system of speech is the on-stage presence or absence of the speaker. This variable has an impact similar to that of the on-stage presence or absence of the puppet-operator. When the speaker is present, the speech-signs of the puppet are radically transformed from wherever they might otherwise be on the continuum of representation to a location toward the conceptual end of the continuum. The on-stage presence of the speaker differs from that of the puppet-operator, however, in that it is commonly employed not only with imitative speech-signs, as is the presence of the puppet-operator with imitative design-signs, but with speech-signs from both ends of the continuum, operating in a different manner for each.

We have seen how Jurkowski rails against synchronic approaches that fail to recognize the element of service. What is actually at issue, however, is not service, but the interaction, or lack thereof, between the on-stage speaker and the puppet. In Jurkowski's example of Master Pedro's puppet theatre, the story-teller does not verbally interact with the puppets, and delivers all of the speech in the performance, be it narrative or character-speech. A similar lack of interaction obtains in our Japanese example. Although Jurkowski argues that Bunraku puppets differ from Master Pedro's because they "are not simply illustrations to accompany the storyteller's chanting . . . [but] are visual components of the characters" (1988 [1983]: 65), the same may be said, as we have seen, of Master Pedro's puppets, for they, too, "are not simply illustrations." The "Petrushka" show to which Jurkowski refers, however, as well as our example from India, have on-stage speakers who verbally interact with the puppets, translating their voice-modified speech and engaging in dialogue. Proschan writes: "Significantly, in many of the cases cited, the voice modifiers are found in use along with an interpreter or interlocutor. The interlocutor may employ a peculiar form of dialogue which involves his or her repetition, often in the form of questions, of the puppet's distorted statements" (1981: 533). As Jurkowski insists, this is surely a different matter.

Noninteractive on-stage speakers, as in Master Pedro's show and in our Japanese example, deliver character-speech that tends toward the imitative end of the continuum. If they were to interact with the puppets, speaking for themselves in normal voices, they would blur the line that distinguishes puppet speech from human speech. The speech-signs they deliver are conceptual in that the audience can clearly see that the puppet is incapable of speaking for itself. Conversely, interactive on-stage speakers, or interlocutors, as in the "Petrushka" show and in our Indian example, deliver human speech of their own, set against the voice-modified speech of the puppets. The line between the two kinds of speech remains quite clear. The puppet's speech is already conceptual in itself, as it is scarcely intelligible, and the on-stage presence of the speaker reinforces this conceptuality by demonstrating its need for translation.

CODA—METAPHOR AND
THE PUPPET

The puppet is involved with metaphor in two distinct yet related ways: the puppet itself can be taken to be a metaphor of humanity, and the term "puppet" can be applied to particular people. The puppet's central process of double-vision, and the ontological paradox of the puppet that follows from this process, is the key to understanding both of these involvements of the puppet and metaphor.

The power of the puppet as a metaphor is an implicit confirmation of the idea that double-vision is the central process to the puppet. In much puppetry, as we have seen, the operator and/or speaker is not present on-stage, and yet the puppet is perceived to be an intentional creation subjected to intentional control. Even when the puppet is presented in the most imitative manner possible, it is perceived by its audience to be an object. As we have also seen, even when the operator and/or speaker is present on-stage, and the puppet is obviously an intentional creation subjected to intentional control, it is still imagined by the audience to have a spurious life. The puppet takes on its metaphorical connotation because it inherently provokes the process of double-vision, creating doubt as to its ontological status: what is the nature of its being?

It will be recalled that the appeal of the puppet has been traced back, alternately, to the fond reminiscence of childhood dolls and to the archetypal tug of the religious totem. As was demonstrated earlier, these theories are individually inadequate and mutually incompatible. All the same, both theories are given new meaning when the concept of double-vision is applied to them. For in both childhood doll-play and in ritual ceremony, there is a marked, and somewhat intentional, tendency for the margin between "object" and "life" to be made unclear; in both, the metaphorical associations of creation and control can easily turn from the question of the puppet's ontology to that of human ontology.

It should not be surprising that the metaphorical relationship of god/person to person/puppet finds far more literary expression than that of child/toy to person/puppet, in that the philosophical ramifications of the former seem far more profound than those of the latter. But as we discuss literary allusions to this metaphorical relationship, the reader should be aware of how easily it translates into the more domestic relationship as well. The puppet's process of double-vision allows it metaphorical power that extends in both directions from humanity.

Batchelder cuts right to the point when she states: "The idea of the puppet is itself ironical. Here is a character, more or less closely related to life, moved about by a human being who is its master. No one misses the analogy between the puppet dominated by man, and man dominated by forces greater than himself" (1947: 299).

This study has repeatedly suggested that the puppet is perceived to be an object, while imagined to have life. The puppet as metaphor of humanity, however, is predicated on an inversion of this formulation. In the metaphorical sense, people are perceived by other people to have life, while, at the same time, they are imagined to be but objects. The power of the puppet as a metaphor of humanity depends on this inversion, and on the ontological paradox that remains. Ultimately, it is a question of who, or what, creates and controls.

Aristotle, or the ancient writer of a text attributed to him, invokes the metaphor of the puppet to explain the gods' control not only over humanity, but over all of the universe. He writes, of the Prime Mover: "All that is necessary is an act of his will—the same as that which controls the marionettes by pulling a string to move the heads or the hands of these little beings, then their shoulders, their eyes, and sometimes all the parts of their bodies, which respond with grace" (quoted in Baird 1965: 38). The universe itself, which is perceived to be real, is imagined in this cosmological metaphor to be but the puppet of a greater force, the original force.

A view no less cosmological, but more focused on the god/person person/puppet metaphor, is current in Java, where, as Brandon informs us, "on a mystical level, the [shadow] screen may be said to symbolize heaven; the banana-log stage, earth; the puppets, man; and the [puppet-operator], god, who through his knowledge and spiritual power brings man to life" (1970: 18).

Jurkowski has discovered an Anatolian poet of the thirteenth century by the name of Birri who similarly expresses the metaphor of humanity as a puppet, created and controlled by the greater force of God:

> Wise man seeking for truth
>   Look up at the tent of the sky
>   Where the Great Showman of the world
>   Has long ago set up his Shadow Theatre.
>   Behind his screen he is giving a show
>   Played by the shadows of men and women of his creation.
>
>   (1988 [1979]: 2)

Perhaps the most extensive meditation in Western poetry on the puppet as a metaphor of humanity may be found in Conrad Aiken's lengthy poem "Punch, the Immortal Liar." Toward the end of the work, the puppet-artist, called the "mountebank," has a moment of reflection:

> Suddenly, there, as he stood at the darkening window [. . .]
>   He saw himself,—though a god,—the puppet of gods;
>   Revolving in antics the dream of a greater dreamer[. . . .]

He addresses one of his puppets:

> "I, too, am a puppet. And as you are a symbol for me [. . .]
>   So I am a symbol, a puppet drawn out upon strings,
>   Helpless, well-coloured, with a fixed and unchanging expression
>   (As though one said 'heartache' or 'laughter'!) of some one who leans
>   Above me, as I above you. . . . And even this Some one,—

Who knows what compulsion he suffers, what hands out of darkness
Play sharp chords upon him! . . . Who knows if those hands are not
ours!"

(Aiken 1953: 360–62)

The chain of ontological doubt suggested in this poem extends upward
from the puppet to the puppet-artist to the "Some one" above, who
himself suffers the "compulsion" of "hands out of darkness." Surprisingly, the poem also suggests that the chain extends downward, and
that the puppet-artist may in some way control the god, and the puppet, in some way, control the puppet-artist.

This last suggestion might seem outrageous, but the puppet does, in
a sense, control the manner in which it is controlled. Craig states, as a
principle of puppet-operation: "You don't move it, you let it move;
that's the art" (quoted in Jurkowski 1988 [1979]: 14). In the practical
sense, this means that the role of the puppet-operator is to learn the
movement potential of the puppet, and to allow for that potential to be
realized. In a more mystical sense, although one's threshold for such
mysticism might easily be transgressed, it means that the puppet-operator's role is to show humility in the presence of his or her creation.

Similarly, Philpott notes the contention of Walter Wilkinson, a nineteenth-century English puppeteer and author, that "the idea that puppets are inanimate creatures controlled by human beings is incorrect
and that the position is exactly the opposite: the showman is at the
mercy of his puppets" (1969: 209). The suggestion, in Wilkinson's
ironic contention as in Aiken's quite serious poem, is not only that the
puppet, the person, and the god all possess an ontologically doubtful
status in being controlled by the next greater force, but that their ontological status is no less doubtful in being controlled by the next *lesser*
force. The metaphorical paradox of the puppet can cut in both directions.

The gods' creation and control of humanity is not the only subject of
creation and control offered by the metaphor of the puppet; people, in
various ways, can also be created and controlled by other, more powerful, people. Horace, in his *Satires,* writes, one person to the next:

> . . . what am I to you?
> Look how you who lord it over me
> Bow and scrape for others like a puppet on a string!
>
> (quoted in Jurkowski 1988 [1979]: 2)

The chain of ontological doubt is here identified, metaphorically, within the context of human relations, which may themselves be seen as nothing more than a series of puppetlike trivialities. Speaight notes that Marcus Aurelius presents "a concentrated and scornful picture of the vain show in which the lives of most men are passed [when he writes of] 'a procession's vain pomp, plays on a stage . . . scurrying of startled mice, marionettes dancing on strings' " (1990 [1955]: 26).

Stalberg cites Xuan-zong, an eighth-century emperor of China, who offers a similar picture of the vanity of human life, identifying himself as a pathetic string marionette:

> With carved wood and stretched silk threads, this old man is made,
> With aged skin chicken-like and hair like a crane's, he is just like a
> real man;
> In a moment, the manipulation finished, he lies still and at rest—
> Just like man's life within this world of dreams.
>
> (1984: 21)

The metaphor of the puppet can also be employed in a more internalized sense. Within any given person, the ontological status of the "face" presented to other people may be subjected, metaphorically, to doubt. Jurkowski points to Adam Mickiewicz, a Polish Romantic, who writes: "These artificial marionettes we call people may embrace us in friendship, smile at us, cry sometimes, but underneath you find egoism, greed and pride manipulating their strings, dominating these figures" (1988 [1979]: 6).

The metaphorical linkages of humanity to the puppet have been expressed not only in literature, but in the theatre itself. As Batchelder remarks:

> Some types of poetic or tragic drama are suitable for puppets.
> Maeterlinck's *The Death of Tintagiles* proved an excellent puppet me-

dium, partly because of its concentrated intensity, and partly because the characters are so obviously in the power of forces beyond their control that they seem like human puppets. (1947: 300–301)

In her analysis of Maeterlinck's work, Knapp comments that "what impressed Maeterlinck . . . was the passive, remote, impersonal and automatonlike nature of the marionette as it fruitlessly confronted the forces of destiny. He saw an analogy between man and marionette: both are manipulated by outer forces, both are unaware of this control over their lives" (1975: 77).

There is certainly great power in this metaphorical usage of the puppet, but it should be noted that such usage does not work equally well with all types of puppets. When a pair of hand-puppets engage in an awkward and unlikely embrace, or a group of Sicilian rod-marionettes joyfully bash at one another until heads literally roll, the rather melancholy metaphor of humanity as slave to destiny seems difficult to apply.

It should also be noted that the second part of Maeterlinck's analogy, that neither the person nor the puppet is aware of being controlled, is inaccurate. Puppets can easily deploy signs to suggest that they are "aware" of being controlled. Jurkowski notes that in a sketch by the contemporary German puppet-artist Albrecht Roser and his marionette clown, Gustav, Gustav's control strings become intentionally entangled, and the puppet appeals to its operator for help in sorting them out; "he is a puppet playing upon his awareness of being a puppet" (1988 [1983]: 78). And it need scarcely be mentioned that many people have an intense feeling of being manipulated by some force greater than themselves, be this a deity, or historical circumstance, or other persons. It might well be argued that the knowledge that human life is itself regularly, if not always, subject to control lends the metaphor of the puppet its peculiar power: we see ourselves in the puppet because we are all too well aware that our freedom of action is circumscribed by external forces.

As suggested in Aiken's poem, the metaphor of the puppet is richer and more complex than it might first appear to be. This richness and complexity is manifested in a production of Prokofiev's "Classical Symphony" by the Budapest State Puppet Theatre, in which the audience watches "live spectators" watch as a "live orchestra" plays the music for a puppet show:

> On a Rococo court stage (the stage within the stage), the puppets present a traditional Italian comedy with rigid conventionality. The courtly, contrived boredom is, however, broken again and again by the appearance of a [puppet] cat on the stage within the stage. At its sight, a pampered lap-dog [belonging to a "spectator" and presumably alive in its own right] grows wild and starts fighting. The two animals chasing each other gradually destroy this contrived world of art. Flies are torn down, wings collapse, instruments fall apart to reveal their mechanical components in the orchestra pit; even a white-wigged spectator [whom we have seen as live] tumbles down and reveals that he is nothing but a termite-eaten empty shell, an empty puppet. (Gál 1978: 41)

By the apocalyptic end of the performance, the audience's understanding of what is and is not real has been thoroughly confused. The question of who is in control has been raised in an unanswerable manner, and the audience has been invited to apply the metaphor of the puppet not only to the "reality" of the performance, but to reality itself.

This brief conspectus of literary and theatrical employments of the puppet as metaphor suggests that the metaphor might well be as widespread as the phenomenon of the puppet itself, and might be operative, as is the process of double-vision, in a synchronic manner. That is, it might well be that the metaphor of the puppet is as pervasive in human thought as the phenomenon of the puppet is in human theatre. A fascinating question arises from this suggestion: does the metaphor follow from observation of the puppet, or does the puppet follow from recognition of the metaphor? Or, to put the question differently: does the sense that people and puppets are alike in being created and controlled by greater forces follow from the observation that the puppet is, indeed, so created and controlled, or does the practice of creating and controlling puppets follow from the observation that people are so created and controlled? It is doubtful that this question can be answered with any certainty, and no attempt to do so will be made here. But the question itself is significant, in that it presents at least the possibility that humanity, believing itself to be created and controlled by a more powerful force, needs to give expression to this belief by creating and controlling what amount to surrogate people, in a fashion analogous to that in which a child, subject to the discipline of parents, exercises a childish discipline upon dolls.

Whether the metaphor of the puppet or the puppet itself came first, the puppet's performance cannot help but raise metaphorical implications. As we have seen, these implications extend beyond the immediately obvious matter of creation and control. As Szilágyi contends, "The true means of expression of puppetry is . . . the stage metaphor":

> With its symbolic style of performance the puppet stage makes the spectator believe that while the theatrical world may be on a separate plane, one on which the puppets are independent beings obeying their own laws, everything ultimately is rooted in the human world and therefore reflected. . . . [The spectator] is reminded that the unreal world of art and the reality of everyday life exist simultaneously and alongside one another. (1967 [1965]: 37)

It is not just a question of creation and control that the metaphor of the puppet raises through the process of double-vision, but a question of comprehending reality itself: what is an "object," what is "life"?

The distinction drawn earlier between the puppet and the live actor can be seen clearly in these metaphorical references to the puppet: the figure of the live actor cannot sustain metaphors such as these, because it does not invite such profound questions of creation and control, and does not challenge the audience with the perplexing ontological paradox of double-vision, "object" versus "life."

The puppet is also involved with the idea of metaphor in that the term "puppet" may be applied, metaphorically, to particular people. When it is, it is not applied as a term of approbation.

The term itself, even aside from its metaphorical application, has become an unhappy one, at least in the West. Its connotations might not be inherently pejorative in cultures with traditions of puppetry that are highly valued; but in the West, where puppet traditions are generally taken to be marginal derivations of live theatre, these connotations are almost invariably negative.

Facing up to this reality, Craig writes: " 'Puppet' is a term of contempt, though there still remain some who find beauty in these little figures, degenerate though they have become" (1911: 90). Of course, even Craig betrays a certain contempt for "these little figures," arguing that being degenerate, they must be superseded by the more exalted figure of the Übermarionette.

If it should seem that Craig overstates the matter when he writes that " 'puppet' is a term of contempt," or if it should seem that, decades later, the term would be accorded a bit more respect, one need only consider Malkin's measured response to the September 1972 "Puppet" issue of *The Drama Review*:

> The editors go so far as to put the word *puppet* in quotation marks because the word, in their view, does not "describe satisfactorily . . . the concepts of the inanimate actor, depersonalization, incarnation, and so forth" [Michael Kirby, "Introduction," *Drama Review* 16 (1972): 3]. It is as though the editors were convinced that the word *puppet*, without quotation marks, represents too elementary a concept or too naive an art form for their purposes. They seem to ignore or be ignorant of the possibility that the puppet, like the actor and the mask, is an essential element of the theatre. The articles treat the puppet as mask, the puppet as symbol, the actor as puppet and so forth, but there is no attempt to articulate any contemporary concept of the puppet as puppet. (1975: 3)

And if it be thought that this condescension has lessened with the passing of nearly two more decades, the reader is invited to reflect upon the number and the nature of discussions about puppetry he or she might have had with any adult who did not have a scholarly or practical interest in puppet theatre.

It might well be that the denigration of puppetry derives in part from the metaphorical associations that the puppet evokes. In the contemporary West, religious ritual is often viewed with only slightly less condescension than childhood play. And, as puppetry in the West has been reduced, by and large, to scholarly studies of puppetry in the religions of other cultures, and to performances for children in this culture, this condescension has amply been reinforced. It would seem, if one may speculate for a moment, that sophisticated Westerners have an almost morbid fear of taking the power of their imagination as seriously as the power of their perception. They find the juxtaposition of perception and imagination, with the ensuing ontological paradox that threatens their understanding of "object" and "life," to be unnerving, and they therefore avoid the problem entirely by condescending to the practice of puppetry that raises it. Perhaps a culture's willingness to appreciate puppetry depends on that culture's willingness to accept the challenging ontological paradox of double-vision.

To speak of a person, metaphorically, as a puppet is to speak of that person with a certain degree of contempt. This contempt is rooted in the contempt in which the term itself is held, but is even more complex. To be called a puppet is not only to be labeled with an unpleasant term, but is also to have one's ontological status subjected to contemptuous doubt. A full examination of the ways in which the term puppet has been applied to people is beyond the scope of this study; but two common applications can be discussed.

Certain politicians, and, indeed, certain governments, are regularly called puppets. For example, Vidkun Quisling, a man whose very name has become part of the English language, was called a puppet of the Nazis when they established him in power over conquered Norway; also, the government established by the Vietnamese in conquered Cambodia was called a "puppet regime." The contempt in being denominated a puppet is obvious; but beneath that contempt is an attack upon the ontological status of the subject. Did Quisling and the Vietnamese regime govern in their own right, or were they created and controlled by forces, in these cases political in nature, more powerful than themselves? Were they "objects" acted upon, or "lives" that act? Both Quisling and the Vietnamese regime in Cambodia did, in fact, govern ostensibly independent nations; but at the same time, both were obviously responsive to the will of those who established them in power. Their ontological status was certainly in doubt; metaphorically, they were puppets in every sense.

Likewise, men or women in love are regularly called puppets. Let us take as our example Cleopatra, a figure of history and literature who is frequently believed to have been in the thrall of not just a few particular men, but of love itself. Although, both in history and in literature, Cleopatra is accepted as a person with no less life than any other person, she is, at the same time, seen to be an object responsive to the overwhelming power of romance. Thus Cleopatra is a "puppet of love," created and controlled by a force, in this case emotional in nature, more powerful than herself. Again, her ontological status is in doubt, and, metaphorically, she too is a puppet in every sense.

It is important to recognize that while such terms as the "puppet governor" and the "puppet of love" involve questions of creation and control, they imply the presence of what may be called a "world-audience" that must make something of the ontological status of the person under question. As with the puppet as a general metaphor of humanity, what is at issue is nothing less than the question of one's status as "object" and/or as "life."

The power of the puppet, as a metaphor of humanity and as a term applied to people, arises out of the paradoxical process of double-vision, which is central to the puppet. The theatrical audience and the world-audience must grapple, ultimately, with matters of ontology, with matters of being. The puppet-stage and the world-stage present figures that are a challenge to comprehend; it is the task of their audiences, which are nothing less than humanity, in part or in whole, to arbitrate the nature of being.

WORKS CITED

Adachi, Barbara (1985). *Backstage at Bunraku.* New York: Weatherhill.

Aiken, Conrad (1953). "Punch: The Immortal Liar." *Collected Poems.* New York: Oxford University Press.

Arnott, Peter D. (1964). *Plays Without People: Puppetry and Serious Drama.* Bloomington: Indiana University Press.

Baird, Bil (1965). *The Art of the Puppet.* New York: Macmillan.

Batchelder, Marjorie H. (1947). *Rod-Puppets and the Human Theatre.* Columbus: Ohio State University Press.

Beaumont, Cyril (1958). *Puppets and Puppetry.* New York: Studio Publications.

Blackham, Olive (1948). *Puppets into Actors.* London: W. Taylor.

Bocek, Jaroslav (1963). *Jiří Trnka: Artist and Puppet Master.* Trans. Till Gottheiner. Prague: Artia.

Bogatyrev, Petr (1976 [1938]). "Semiotics in the Folk Theatre." Trans. Bruce Kochis. In *Semiotics of Art,* 33–50. See Matejka and Titunik 1976.

——— (1983 [1973]). "The Interconnection of Two Similar Semiotic Systems: The Puppet Theatre and the Theatre of Living Actors." Trans. Milanne S. Hahn. *Semiotica* 47-1/4: 47–68.

Böhmer, Gunther (1971 [1969]). *The Wonderful World of Puppets.* Trans. Gerald Morice. Boston: Plays, Inc.

Brandon, James R. (1970). *On Thrones of Gold: Three Javanese Shadow Plays.* Cambridge, MA: Harvard University Press.

——— (1975). *Kabuki: Five Classic Plays.* Cambridge, MA: Harvard University Press.

Brecht, Stefan (1988). *Peter Schumann's Bread and Puppet Theatre.* 2 vols. New York: Routledge, Chapman and Hall.

Brown, Bob (1980). Personal interview with author, September 11.

Carlson, Marvin (1984). *Theories of the Theatre: A Historical and Critical Survey, From the Greeks to the Present.* Ithaca, NY: Cornell University Press.

Cho, Oh-Kon (1979). *Korean Puppet Theatre: Kkoktu Kaksi.* East Lansing, MI: Asian Studies Center.

—— (1988). *Traditional Korean Theatre.* Berkeley, CA: Asian Humanities Press.

Coleridge, Samuel Taylor (1951 [1817]). "Biographia Literaria, Chapter XIV." In *The Great Critics: An Anthology of Literary Criticism,* edited by James Harry Smith and Edd Winfield Parks, 526–43. 3rd ed. New York: Norton.

Craig, E. Gordon (1911). *On the Art of the Theatre.* New York: Theatre Arts Books.

Currell, David (1987 [1985]). *The Complete Book of Puppet Theatre.* Totowa, NJ: Barnes and Noble.

Efimova, Nina (1935). *Adventures of a Russian Puppet Theatre.* Trans. Elena Mitcoff. Birmingham: Puppetry Imprints.

Elam, Keir (1980). *The Semiotics of Theatre and Drama.* New York: Methuen.

Engler, Larry, and Carol Fijan (1973). *Making Puppets Come Alive.* New York: Taplinger Publishing.

Eynat-Confino, Irene (1987). *Beyond the Mask: Gordon Craig, Movement, and the Actor.* Carbondale: Southern Illinois University Press.

Foote, Samuel (1812). "Piety in Pattens." *Biographia Dramatica, or A Companion to the Playhouse.* Vol. 3. London: Longman, Hurst, Rees, Orme, and Brown.

Gál, Péter Molnár (1978). "Theatre with Puppets." In *Hungarian Puppet Theatre,* 13–51. See Szilágyi 1978.

Gerdjikov, Stantscho (1967 [1965]). "A New Art Is Born." In *Puppet Theatre,* 42–43. See UNIMA and Niculescu 1967 (1965).

Glore, John (1980). "Midsummer Animations: The 1980 World Puppetry Festival." *Theatre* 12.1: 56–64.

Gould, Stephen Jay (1989). *Wonderful Life: The Burgess Shale and the Nature of History.* New York: W. W. Norton.

Green, Thomas A., and W. J. Pepicello (1983). "Semiotic Interrelationships in the Puppet Play." *Semiotica* 47–1/4: 147–61.

Gross, Joan (1987). "The Form and Function of Humour in the Liège Puppet Theatre." In *Humor and Comedy,* 47–54. See Scherzer and Scherzer 1987.

Halász, László (1978). "The Puppet Theatre and its Public Seen by the Psychologist." In *Hungarian Puppet Theatre,* 59–64. See Szilágyi 1978.

Henson Associates (1980). *The Art of the Muppets.* New York: Bantam Books.

Jones, John (1980 [1962]). *On Aristotle and Greek Tragedy.* Stanford, CA: Stanford University Press.

Jurkowski, Henryk (1967 [1965]). "The Eternal Conflict." In *Puppet Theatre,* 25–27. See UNIMA and Niculescu 1967 (1965).

—— (1988 [1978]). "The Language of the Contemporary Puppet Theatre." In *Aspects,* 51–56. See Jurkowski 1988.

—— (1988 [1979]). "Literary Views on the Puppet Theatre." In *Aspects,* 1–36. See Jurkowski 1988.

—— (1988 [1983]). "The Sign Systems of Puppetry." In *Aspects,* 57–84. See Jurkowski 1988.

—— (1988 [1984]). "Towards a Theatre of Objects." In *Aspects,* 37–44. See Jurkowski 1988.

—— (1988). *Aspects of the Puppet Theatre: A Collection of Essays.* Ed. Penny Francis. London: Puppetry Centre Trust.

—— (1990). "Keynote Address." *A Propos* (Fall, 1990): 16–19.

Kaplin, Stephen (1989). "Signs of Life: An Analysis of Contemporary Puppet Theatre in New York City." Master's thesis, New York University.

Kleist, Heinrich von (1978 [1810]). "On the Marionette Theatre." Trans. Idris Perry. *Times Literary Supplement,* 20 Oct. 1978: 1211–12.

Knapp, Bettina (1975). *Maurice Maeterlinck.* Ed. Sylvia Bowman. Twayne's World Authors Series. Boston: Twayne Publishers.

Kolár, Erik (1964). "Aesthetic Roots of the Czech Puppet Theatre." *Divaldo* 14 (January): 67–71.

—— (1967 [1965]). "The Puppet Theatre: A Form of Visual or Dramatic Art?" In *Puppet Theatre,* 31–32. See UNIMA and Niculescu 1967 (1965).

Kott, Jan (1976). "Bunraku and Kabuki, or, About Imitation." *Salmagundi* 35: 99–109.

Kroó, György (1978). "Music Charmed into a Living Spectacle." In *Hungarian Puppet Theatre,* 52–58. See Szilágyi 1978.

Lee, Miles (1958). *Puppet Theatre: Production and Manipulation.* London: Faber and Faber.

Lenkisch, Stefan (1967 [1965]). "The Puppet as a Poetic Symbol." In *Puppet Theatre,* 27–29. See UNIMA and Niculescu 1967 (1965).

McPharlin, Paul (1938). "Aesthetic of the Puppet Revival." Master's Thesis, Wayne State University.

—— (1949). *The Puppet Theatre in America: A History.* New York: Harper & Brothers.

Magnin, Charles (1862). *Histoire des Marionnettes en Europe depuis l'Antiquité jusqu'a nos Jours.* 2nd ed. Paris: Michel Lévy Frères.

Malík, Jan (1967 [1965]). "Tradition and the Present Day." In *Puppet Theatre*, 7–14. See UNIMA and Niculescu 1967 (1965).

Malkin, Michael R. (1975). "A Critical Perspective on Puppetry as Theatre Art." *Puppetry Journal* 27.1: 3–8.

―――― (1977). *Traditional and Folk Puppets of the World.* New York: A. S. Barnes.

―――― (1980). *Puppets: Art and Entertainment.* Washington, D.C.: Puppeteers of America.

Martin, Louise (1945). "The Chicago Little Theatre Marionettes 1915–1917." *Puppetry 1944–1945: An International Yearbook.* Vol. 15: 4–6.

Matejka, Ladislav, and Irwin R. Titunik, eds. (1976). *Semiotics of Art: Prague School Contributions.* Cambridge, MA: MIT Press.

Messenger, John C. (1971). "Ibibio Drama." *Africa* 41.3 (July): 207–222.

Meyerhold, Vsevelod E. (1969 [1913]). *Meyerhold on Theatre.* Trans. Edward Braun. New York: Hill and Wang.

Milovsoroff, Basil (1976). "Random Reflections on Puppets and Art." *Puppetry Journal* 28.3: 3–5.

Myrsiades, Linda (1988). *The Karagiozis Heroic Performance in Greek Shadow Theatre.* Trans. Kostas Myrsiades. Hanover, NH: University Press of New England.

Obraztsov, Sergei (1950). *My Profession.* Trans. Ralph Parker and Valentina Scott. Moscow: Foreign Languages Publishing House.

―――― (1954). *Puppets and the Puppet Theatre.* London: Society for Cultural Relations with the USSR.

―――― (1967 [1965]). "Some Considerations on the Puppet Theatre." In *Puppet Theatre*, 17–21. See UNIMA and Niculescu 1967 (1965).

―――― (1985 [1981]). *My Profession.* 2nd ed. Trans. Doris Bradbury. Moscow: Raduga Publishers.

Pasqualino, Antonio (1987). "Humor and Puppets." In *Humor and Comedy*, 8–29. See Scherzer and Scherzer 1987.

Philpott, A. R. (1969). *Dictionary of Puppetry.* Boston: Plays, Inc.

Proschan, Frank (1980). "The Puppet Traditions of Sub-Saharan Africa: Descriptions and Definitions." Undergraduate Honors Thesis, University of Texas, Austin.

―――― (1981). "Puppet Voices and Interlocutors: Language in Folk Puppetry." *Journal of American Folklore* 94 (347): 527–55.

―――― (1983). "The Semiotic Study of Puppets, Masks, and Performing Objects." *Semiotica* 47-1/4: 3–44.

———— (1987). "The Cocreation of the Comic in Puppetry." In *Humor and Comedy*, 30–46. See Sherzer and Sherzer 1987.

Roccoberton, Bart, Jr. (1982). Personal interview with author, January 8.

Samar, D. L. (1960). "Puppets and Puppeteers of Rajasthan." In *Puppet Theatre Around the World*, edited by Som Benegal, 64–70. New Delhi: Caxton Press.

Schwartz, Bruce (1983). "Working with Puppets: Bruce Schwartz, Theodora Skipateres, Julie Taymor." Interviews by C. Lee Janner. *Performing Arts Journal* 7.1: 103–116.

Sherzer, Dina, and Joel Sherzer, eds. (1987). *Humor and Comedy in Puppetry: Celebration in Popular Culture*. Bowling Green, OH: Bowling Green State University Popular Press.

Siegel, Harro (1967 [1965]). "Actor and Puppeteer." In *Puppet Theatre*, 21–24. See UNIMA and Niculescu 1967 (1965).

Soroky, Rose (1982). "The Aesthetics of Puppetry." *Puppetry Journal* 23.5: 3–7.

Spatharis, Sotiris (1976 [1960]). *Behind the White Screen*. Trans. Mario Rinvolucri and Leslie Finer. New York: Red Dust.

Speaight, George (1947). "Puppet Voices." *Puppetry 1946–1947: An International Yearbook*. Vol. 16: 37–39.

———— (1990 [1955]). *The History of the English Puppet Theatre*. 2nd ed. Carbondale: Southern Illinois University Press.

Stalberg, Roberta Helmer (1984). *China's Puppets*. San Francisco: China Books.

Symons, Arthur (1909). *Plays, Acting, and Music*. New York: E. P. Dutton.

Szilágyi, Dezső (1967 [1965]). "The Modern Puppet Stage and Its Audience." In *Puppet Theatre*, 35–38. See UNIMA and Niculescu 1967 (1965).

Szilágyi, Dezső, ed. (1978). *Contemporary Hungarian Puppet Theatre*. Trans. Elisabeth Hoch. Budapest: Corvina.

Taymor, Julie (1983). "Working with Puppets: Bruce Schwartz, Theodora Skipateres, Julie Taymor." Interviews by C. Lee Janner. *Performing Arts Journal* 7.1: 103–116.

Ulbricht, H. (1970). *Wayang Purwa: Shadows of the Past*. Kuala Lumpur: Oxford University Press.

UNIMA (Union Internationale de la Marionnette) and Margaret Niculescu, eds. (1967 [1965]). *The Puppet Theatre of the Modern World*. Trans. Ewald Osers and Elizabeth Strick. Boston: Plays, Inc.

Veltruský, Jiří (1964 [1940]). "Man and Object in the Theater." In *A Prague School Reader on Esthetics, Literary Structure, and Style*, edited and translated by Paul L. Garvin, 83–91. Washington, D.C.: Georgetown University Press.

——— (1976). "Contribution to the Semiotics of Acting." In *Sound, Sign and Meaning*, Michigan Slavic Contributions 6, edited by Ladislav Matejka, 553–606. Ann Arbor: University of Michigan Press.

——— (1983). "Puppetry and Acting." *Semiotica* 47-1/4: 69–122.

INDEX

About the Author

STEVE TILLIS, playwright, performer, and director, has worked professionally in the theatre since 1974. His article "The Appeal of the Puppet: God or Toy?" was published in *The Language of the Puppet*, edited by Laurence R. Kominz and Mark Levinson.

Printed in the USA
CPSIA information can be obtained
at www.ICGtesting.com
LVHW020847131023
760813LV00006B/529